PERFORMING ARCHITECTURE

PERFORMING ARCHITECTURE

OPERA HOUSES, THEATRES
AND CONCERT HALLS FOR
THE TWENTY-FIRST CENTURY

First published 2006
by Merrell Publishers Limited

Head Office:
81 Southwark Street
London SE1 0HX

New York Office:
49 West 24th Street, 8th Floor
New York, NY 10010

merrellpublishers.com

Publisher Hugh Merrell
Editorial Director Julian Honer
US Director Joan Brookbank
Sales and Marketing Manager Kim Cope
Sales and Marketing Executive Amina Arab
Co-editions Manager Anne Le Moigne
Assistant Manager, US Sales and Marketing
  Elizabeth Choi
Managing Editor Anthea Snow
Project Editors Claire Chandler,
  Rosanna Fairhead
Editor Helen Miles
Art Director Nicola Bailey
Designer Paul Shinn
Production Manager Michelle Draycott
Production Controller Sadie Butler

British Library Cataloguing-in-Publication Data:
Hammond, Michael
Performing architecture : opera houses, theatres
and concert halls for the twenty-first century
1.Theater architecture 2.Theaters 3.Music-halls
I.Title
725.8'1

ISBN-13: 978-1-8589-4279-7
ISBN-10: 1-8589-4279-9

Produced by Merrell Publishers Limited
Copy-edited by Rosanna Fairhead and
  Catherine Langford
Proof-read by Sarah Yates
Designed by Dennis Bailey

Printed and bound in China

Front cover: Walt Disney Concert Hall (Gehry
Partners), see pp. 116–19
Back cover: Verizon Hall, Kimmel Center for the
Performing Arts (Rafael Viñoly), see pp. 42–47
Pages 2–3: Elbe Philharmonic Hall (Herzog
& de Meuron), see pp. 210–13
Pages 6–7: Esplanade National Performing
Arts Centre (Michael Wilford & Partners), see
pp. 65–67
Pages 10–11: Liquidrom, New Tempodrom
(Von Gerkan, Marg & Partner), see pp. 48–51
Pages 14–15: The Grant Park Orchestra in the
Jay Pritzker Pavilion, Millennium Park (Gehry
Partners), see pp. 86–89
Pages 236–37: The Margot and Bill Winspear
Opera House, Dallas Center for the Performing
Arts (Foster and Partners), see pp. 204–5
Page 240: New Mariinski Theatre (Dominique
Perrault Architecte), see pp. 196–99

CONTENTS

For Annalisa

The foundation for this book was laid very early in my life. My father managed a team of architects designing onshore naval facilities for the UK government, and I grew up surrounded by plans, sections and models. I developed a love of the mysterious drawings on rolls of strange-smelling linen. Many years later, my wife, Annalisa (a former ballet dancer), took me on a surprise tour behind the scenes at Glyndebourne, Michael Hopkins's opera house set in the Sussex countryside. With Annalisa's insight I was introduced to the diverse range of support activities, from wig-making and costume design, through set manufacture, to the unloading of massive trucks with giant lifting gantries. All these activities required unique skills, equipment and, most importantly, dedicated spaces.

Like most people, I had been aware that the design of an auditorium was a specialist affair involving an army of consultants, not least of these, those practising the dark art of acoustics. Wandering around Glyndebourne, however, without there being a performance in progress to distract me, I began to understand the great complexity of designing such a building, and I was impressed.

Shortly after this, I had the opportunity to visit the Brighton Dome Concert Hall during its refurbishment. Once again, I gained insight into the immense challenge the architect faces in order to create the right conditions for a successful performance, both artistically and commercially – in this case in a listed structure.

The book's fate was sealed when I was given a presentation by Rafael Viñoly's London team of the design rationale for the Leicester Performing Arts Centre. The complexities were attacked with such passion by the flamboyant architect, with radical ideas that forced the theatre group to evaluate many of its established practices, that my interest turned to fascination.

I was intrigued by the notion of performing spaces as organisms in their own right, breathing people in like particles into a lung, exposing them to sound, colour, drama and emotion, and exhaling them, enriched, back into the community. I set out to find a book to feed my new-found interest, but was dismayed to find that nothing up-to-date existed. The die for *Performing Architecture* was cast.

Julian Honer, Merrell's editorial director, and his team, Rosie Fairhead and Nicola Bailey, have been extremely supportive during the entire process of realizing this book. The architects whose projects are featured here have also been magnificent in the face of my questioning, badgering and image-hunting. Raj Patel of Arup Acoustics has been very patient with my many requests for background information.

Performing Architecture is not a technical resource or design bible. I hope, however, that it will provide a colourful insight into some of the most exciting work that our leading architects are producing in order to enable those from another creative industry, that of the performing arts, to entertain us in the twenty-first century.

INTRODUCTION

At the beginning of the twenty-first century, the performing-arts industry is being forced through nothing less than a total metamorphosis. Building iconic venues has always been controversial, and the winning of budgets, often from public funds, is an established battle zone. Now, however, new fronts in the fight for survival are emerging that strike at the very heart of the industry: audiences, the lifeblood of the performing arts. Audiences across the globe are both ageing and being wooed by an increasingly sophisticated range of home entertainment. The industry has recently become too dependent on the extended life (and relative wealth) of a core of older patrons. In response to these issues, live performing art is being forced to reinvent itself, and architects have been addressing these challenges with some of the most fascinating buildings of our time.

A vast array of problems faces the designer of a new performing-arts venue in the twenty-first century. The demands on such a building are complex and present considerable challenges in their own right. Add to this the issues of inclusion, globalization and dwindling audiences that have emerged more recently, the old dragons of élitism, funding and iconism, and mix with a dose of changing design trends and increased need for sustainability – these are the key elements in the vast melting pot of a client's brief.

In this book, we explore and illustrate how the great architects of our time have interpreted these challenges, and take a world tour of some of the most exciting performing spaces being designed and built for the twenty-first century.

In some ways it is incredible, considering all the reasons not to build a performing venue, that any get built at all. The process starts with a brief, often influenced by performers focused entirely on their own

needs, which is interpreted by the architect, who naturally wants to add his own personality and ideas to the design. Sometimes decades can elapse between concept and completion. The refurbishment of the Royal Opera House in London took so long, and went so far over its budget, that the very support of its patrons was threatened and it almost had to be halted. Oscar Niemeyer's opera house in São Paulo (pp. 134–35), too, spent fifty years on the drawing board. There are, of course, always exceptions: one is the curious case of the Copenhagen Opera (pp. 94–97), where a single benefactor managed the whole cycle in four years.

Finding a solution to the issue of audience age is crucial to the long-term survival of the performing-arts industry, but there is another problem, apparently separate but in practice very closely linked: that of audience mobility. There was some surprise recently at the English National Opera when it was discovered that two thousand regular audience members have a disability of some kind. Many of these disabilities, though by no means all, are caused by old age. New legislation has sparked the revamping of many established venues, as it is no longer acceptable for an event to be accessible only to those able to climb long flights of stairs. The architects of those projects in this book that are conversions or refurbishments – such as the overhaul of London's Coliseum in 2004 (pp. 82–85) – have had to pay considerable attention to circulation in the planning of their designs.

Many initiatives from venue managers, orchestras and of course architects are testing public reactions, some achieving greater success than others. Inspired by the rise of a new phenomenon, the 'flashmob', in 2003, the BBC created a series of 'off the wall' operas in public places, to try to engage a younger audience. The first,

The beautiful finishes and landmark status of the Copenhagen Opera by Henning Larsens Tegnestue belie the extremely short time it took to design and build the venue.

17

Top: The design of a new
building for South East
Essex College has greatly
increased applications to
the institution.

Bottom: It is hoped that
the inclusive design of
Oslo's National Opera
House, with its swimming
platform, will encourage
the city's young people
to try out opera.

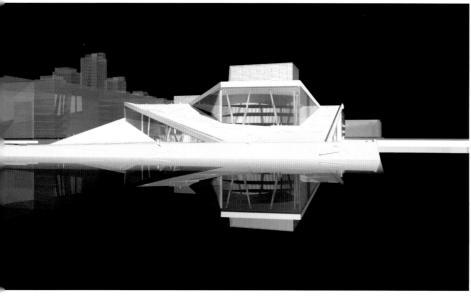

held in London's Paddington Station late in 2004, used a contemporary take on the myth of Orpheus and Eurydice with a passion for football as the theme. Performers even wore football strips, and on the day flashmobbers were invited by text message to participate in the event. It was broadcast on television and proved extremely popular.

It is now recognized that an exciting new building can have a great effect on the number of visitors to a site. South East Essex College, for example, reports an increase of 45 per cent in applications since it built a new facility, complete with theatre, in the centre of Southend (pp. 108–11). Snøhetta's National Opera House in Oslo (pp. 188–91) was designed to appeal directly to a younger generation, and the planned sleek, 'stealth-bomber' lines have indeed been accepted by young Norwegians as 'cool'. To allow more diverse use, the roof of the opera house inclines into the fjord and doubles as a swimming platform. The Unicorn Theatre for Children in London (pp. 140–43) adopts the longer-term approach by creating a theatre that engages children from the age of four in creating performances. Its architect, Keith Williams, believes that "introducing children to high-quality theatre at an early age allows future generations to connect with theatre more widely".

In the form of sophisticated home entertainment, technology is presenting a threat to live performing arts, but it can also be a friend to the architect of such venues. Technical advances have enabled enormous steps forward in the understanding and improvement of acoustics. Even as recently as the 1950s, acoustic design involved almost more guesswork than science. London's Royal Festival Hall is a perfect example of a major performing venue created during this transitory era of acoustic technology, when engineers had some

The New Globe Theater, off Manhattan, will replicate the acoustics of London's Globe.

understanding of the science but lacked the data needed to guarantee the required result. The last few decades have changed all that, and now many of the world's leading venues are using this new-found knowledge as a stimulus for refurbishment, to include radical improvements to the sound quality. (The Royal Festival Hall is being given just such a new lease of life by Allies and Morrison; pp. 170–71.) Whereas the builders of the early concert halls of the eighteenth century used a hit-and-miss process that meant that no one could be certain of a hall's acoustic performance until the building was complete, technology now enables architects to hear the 'sound' of their design before a single brick is laid.

So advanced is today's technology that such specialist firms as Arup Acoustics can effectively bring buildings back from the dead. The Neues Gewandhaus in Leipzig, considered to be acoustically the best concert hall in the world, was bombed by the Allies in 1944 and appeared to be lost forever. But that was not the end of the story. Detailed plans exist for the original construction and in 2003 Arup used its own 'black box' software to re-create the hall as a virtual three-dimensional model. This initially held all the dimensions of the building – not an exceptional fact in itself – but detailed acoustic attributes of every surface in the auditorium, from panelling to seating, were then added to the model: absorption, reflectivity, density and so on. Finally, up-to-date statistical data of audiences, including weight and bulk, and even clothing (which would have varied with the seasons) were added. With all this data, the software could re-create the exact acoustic 'signature' of the hall.

All that was needed then was an orchestra. 'Close' recordings of live performances, where each instrument or section has its own microphone, capture pure sound and do not pick up any of the acoustic characteristics of the recording space. This sound is not what the audience will hear but is simply what the orchestra produces. The pure digital 'orchestra' was then placed in the virtual hall. With this technology, Arup can produce an effect as close to the original as possible. Wearing headphones in its acoustic laboratory in New York, all you have to do is choose your seat and you can be taken back to the early years of the twentieth century to experience the same acoustics as a concert-goer in pre-war Leipzig.

A similar technique will be used to re-create a Shakespearian building in New York, with Foster and Partners' New Globe Theatre (pp. 224–25). The building to be converted, a disused fort on Governor's Island, just off Manhattan, has a similar envelope to that of the Globe Theatre in London. The engineers have captured the digital 'signature' from the original and plan to re-create the exact acoustic performance in its offspring. This level of authenticity can only add value to a new performing-arts venue, providing of course that the original acoustics were worth replicating in the first place.

One would expect, given the sophistication of today's acoustic engineering, that a 'perfect' box would now exist that could be inserted into every new live performance building. Luckily this has not happened; the technology has instead been used to enable the architect to realize more adventurous visions and still have total control over the resulting acoustics. The design of an auditorium requires a very close relationship between the architect and the acoustic engineer. Another aspect that is greatly enhanced by these advances in technology is the flexibility of a venue. Many do not have the luxury of containing several auditoria (Paul Andreu's Oriental Art Centre in Shanghai, pp. 90–93, is one of the lucky ones with its three different halls) but require a high degree of flexibility. The Brighton Dome Concert Hall (pp. 60–63), for example, has to cater in one space for everything from orchestral to rock music. Knowledge of the acoustic demands enables the designer to build in the required flexibility at the concept stage.

Everything in a concert hall affects the acoustics, even the audience's clothes: bulky, heavy winter clothing absorbs more sound than lighter summer garments and can have a significant effect on the reverberation time. When sitting down before a performance, take a moment to reflect on the importance of that apparently simple piece of furniture, the auditorium chair. The seating plays a key role in acoustic design, and is at the root of one major dilemma: the orchestra has to rehearse in an empty auditorium and is heavily reliant on the acoustic feedback to fine-tune the performance, but when it is time for the concert, thousands of people flood into the hall, and the sound characteristics change dramatically. Seating designers are rising to this challenge by striving to create the perfect chair

in acoustic terms, one that has the same level of absorbency whether or not it is occupied.

The seat pitching and spacing also play a big part in the acoustics of a hall. Many influences are at work here, but commercial requirements for once do not conflict with acoustics, as tightly packed seats form a cohesive, solid mass that forms a good barrier. However, cultural differences can intervene and cause problems. The Chinese, for example, are happy for people to come and go during performances, even allowing food (and, to the horror of the acousticians, the use of mobile phones), and when commissioning new buildings they require more space between the seats to allow access without the people adjacent having to stand. This wreaks havoc with the acoustics, as sound can pass between the seats.

The perception that public funds are being spent on 'élitist' buildings has always been an Achilles heel for these projects, leaving them open to attacks from all quarters, and in today's more transparent and politically correct society it is the issue of inclusion more than any other that has influenced the design of contemporary

China's appreciation of and participation in Western classical music is fast increasing. Two buildings to feed this demand are the Oriental Art Centre in Shanghai (left) and the National Grand Theatre of China in Beijing (below left), both designed by Paul Andreu.

Zaha Hadid's dramatic design for an opera house in Cardiff was rejected, and the Wales Millennium Centre, which was expected to appeal to a wider range of people, built in its place.

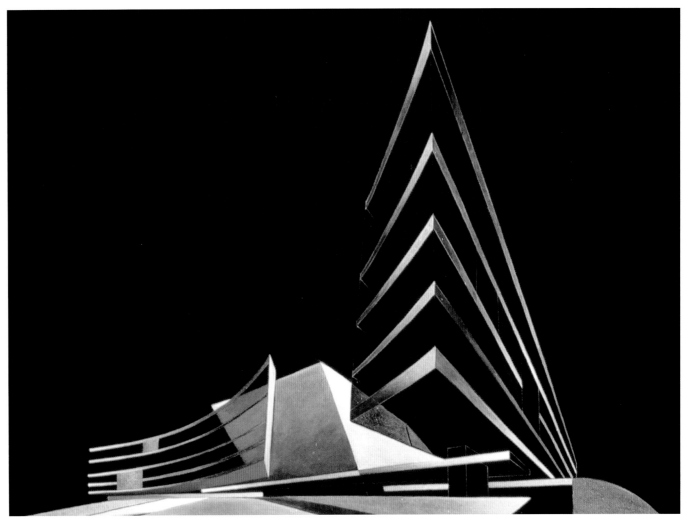

The problems of creating
a performing-arts venue
from an existing building
were solved in very
different ways in Richard
Murphy's Eastgate
Theatre and Arts Centre
(below) and Renzo
Piano's Niccolò Paganini
Auditorium (opposite).

performing spaces. As a result, the performing-arts venue has had to be redefined for the twenty-first century. The new generation of buildings must be part of the public realm, with access to only the core areas being restricted by the requirement for a ticket. These venues include public activities within and around the complex, attracting a wider range of visitors.

The world is still in a state of flux with regard to opera and the vast sums required to realize venues for its performance. No better example of this cultural tension exists than in China. Centuries of tradition and the legacy of a period of Communist oppression are still evident in the new commercial development. It is easy to forget that China is still effectively a police state, although there is still plenty of evidence for this. (During the building of Paul Andreu's Shanghai project, there was no internet access on site, so the project architect had to communicate furtively with Paris HQ at night from her home via a Hotmail account. The internet is still tightly controlled and edited in China, and only recently has access to CNN been allowed.) It is very far, though, from the days of the Cultural Revolution, when dozens of musicians were tortured, murdered or forced to commit suicide at the Shanghai Conservatory, once the foremost centre for Western music in Asia. Then, the piano was condemned as a bourgeois instrument and many pianists had their fingers broken. Contrast this with the fact that China now manufactures more pianos than anywhere else in the world, forcing such established names as Broadwood, Knight and Welmar either to close or to move production to the East. The recent embracing of 'Western' classical music by the Chinese population with its new-found wealth is prompting predictions that China will soon become the world's largest purchaser of classical CDs.

Despite the growing affection for Western classical music, however, even in Beijing, China's capital city, there are bitter debates raging over the enormous opera complex being built by Paul Andreu opposite the Forbidden City (pp. 180–83). Many people believe that the opera will be too expensive for the average person and so will only serve China's new élite. Local architects also believe that their city is becoming a 'playground' of iconic Western architecture in the run-up to the 2008 Olympic Games – such architects as Rem Koolhaas, Herzog & de Meuron, Lord Foster and Zaha Hadid are also working on major projects here. Professor Zhou Rong of the Tsinghua University's School of Architecture

holds a typical view of the new opera complex: "It looks like something that's not from the Earth. It's like a tomb, it goes against the conventions of Chinese architecture."

The Cardiff Opera House fiasco, in which Zaha Hadid's world-class, competition-winning design was rejected at the last moment in favour of the less contentious Wales Millennium Centre (pp. 112–15), shows that even in the UK, one of the traditional centres of excellence in Western classical music, there is some uncomfortable feeling about opera and all that it stands for.

Getting a performing-arts project accepted is all about championing its benefits to the wider community. Many of the projects featured in this book are used as catalysts for urban regeneration. Rafael Viñoly's Leicester Theatre and Performing Arts Centre (pp. 178–79), Foster and Partners' West Kowloon Cultural District (pp. 192–95) and Jakob + MacFarlane's Fanal Theatre in Saint-Nazaire (pp. 160–63) are all examples of how a cultural presence is increasingly seen as a key element in regeneration plans. There are also some innovative examples of existing buildings being renovated for a new function, showing a much more genuine sustainability than many new developments described as sustainable. At one end of the scale is Richard Murphy's tiny Eastgate Theatre in Scotland (pp. 98–101), which is an expert conversion of a disused church. Much grander are Renzo Piano's spectacular Niccolò Paganini Auditorium in Parma (pp. 38–41), created from a disused sugar factory, and Herzog & de Meuron's Elbe Philharmonic Hall in Hamburg (pp. 210–13). In some ways, cramming the technical requirements of a theatre into the confines of a protected building requires more innovation than building a larger venue from scratch.

The opportunity to create a performing-arts venue must rate as a holy grail for architects. Unlike the more conventional types of building, such as offices, housing and even civic architecture, which have to conform to the streetscape, a performing-arts venue can afford to be bold and unusual, to stand out. Indeed, it is expected to. The Sydney Opera House, completed in 1973 and arguably the most recognizable building in the world, set a global precedent. Various examples inspired by the Sydney project can be seen in these pages: Santiago Calatrava's Tenerife Auditorium (pp. 72–77), for example, clearly pays homage to Sydney's great icon of the twentieth century. Its sculptural form set beside the docks can be seen from the hills surrounding the capital, Santa Cruz, and glimpsed from many of its streets.

This freedom of design and licence to be flamboyant can, however, be dangerous. Opera houses, concert halls and theatres are all working buildings with many complex functions to fulfil, and these practicalities are on occasion overshadowed by the architecture. The Sydney Opera House is in fact an excellent example of a brilliant visual design in which not enough consideration was given to the acoustics. Ultimately, these buildings have to perform. Neither can venue managers simply rely on performances themselves to provide a sufficient attraction; the building must create an 'experience' and a 'sense of place' for its increasingly demanding audience. It is with such intangibles that live events can really win against home entertainment. Thought must be given to all aspects of a visit, from the foyers and bars to the facilities and ease of access. Considerations of this kind are more than any others influencing the design of performing spaces at the start of the twenty-first century. Indeed, some architects have addressed these issues so successfully that the stunning spaces around the performance area eclipse the auditorium entirely. Michael Wilford's Esplanade National Performing Arts

Centre in Singapore (pp. 65–67) is one example, with fantastic glazed atria sweeping around the complex allowing spectacular views of the city. The public areas of Paul Andreu's Oriental Art Centre in Shanghai are similarly striking and could well serve as a destination in their own right.

This is a far cry from some examples that were created even as recently as the closing years of the twentieth century. The Bastille Opera in Paris, built in 1989 by Uruguayan architect Carlos Ott, presents a classic illustration of the problems of inclusion that are now being solved. Hemmed in by a triangle of roads, the massive building forms a fort-like edifice rising sharply from the pavement. The entrance leads directly to the foyer barrier. No public space here – opera-goers only – and no hint of the activity inside. How many people will have passed this building day and night, by car and even on foot, and have no idea of the wonderful performances taking place? Even really small projects are now striving to provide more transparency, such as the Eastgate Theatre in Scotland by Richard Murphy. For Rafael Viñoly's Leicester Theatre and Performing Arts Centre this was the main focus of the design. Michael Wilford in Singapore, and Paul Andreu in Beijing and Shanghai, have also gone a long way towards blurring the boundaries.

The buildings illustrated in this book prove that the performing-arts industry is in better health than it has been for many years. Those involved at every stage in the management of performing-arts houses are addressing the current problems successfully, and architects are producing buildings for the enjoyment of the arts that will undoubtedly be the means of attracting more people to participate in cultural activities.

PERFORMING ARCHITECTURE

SHANGHAI GRAND THEATRE
ARTE JEAN-MARIE CHARPENTIER
SHANGHAI, CHINA 1998

By any standards, this building deserves the title 'grand'. Conceived by architects Arte Jean-Marie Charpentier, it embodies on an epic scale Shanghai's enthusiastic embracing of world culture and arts while proclaiming its Chinese heritage in its distinctive form. Located in the political and cultural heart of the city, the theatre fulfils the primary terms of its architectural brief, which was for "an open temple in a large park". The form of the huge roof symbolizes a Chinese treasure bowl; and the building is surrounded by 2000 sq. m (21,500 sq. ft)

of grassland planted with over one hundred species of trees and flowers.

Charpentier has used modern technology in a way that expresses Chinese culture while also demonstrating a unity of decorative exterior and functional interior. Six massive glass-clad columns support the roof, dominating the exterior and adding interest to the façade; but despite their imposing size they are transparent and allow glimpses deep into the building. The glass structures and water features are lit up at night to create a glittering 'crystal palace' effect.

Unashamedly international, the project draws on expertise from many countries. The glazing and lighting are German, the interior design and limestone features American, the chandeliers Austrian, the seating Italian and the stage Japanese. The glazed façade, an unusual feature in China, makes use of a special coloured ceramic material that reduces light transmission into the foyer and reduces heat build-up. The aluminium-clad steel roof is an engineering feat on a grand scale, weighing in at 6075 tonnes, the same weight as the Eiffel Tower.

The vast foyer provides a suitably grand introduction to the theatre complex. Approximately 2000 sq. m (21,500 sq. ft) in area and 18 m (59 ft) high, with four levels, it is an impressive space. The pillars, floor and stairs are constructed from a rare white marble from Greece, 'Crystal White', creating a splendidly light and airy atmosphere. The central feature, however, is the 5-tonne chandelier, 7.35 m (24 ft) tall. Designed in and imported from Austria, fashioned from six panpipe-shaped lamp supports of quartz and Italian crystal, and

illuminated by some three hundred lights, it has been nicknamed 'The Blue Danube'.

The auditorium seats 1100 in the stalls, 300 in the circle and 400 in the upper circle. The ratio of seats in the three levels is designed for the best possible visibility and audibility. The two circles stretch out from the wall and overlap in parallel overhead, and the boxes are located at the sides.

The huge stage, 256 sq. m (2756 sq. ft) in size, features eighteen lifting sections, and is one of the largest in Asia. In combination with the proscenium and wave-shaped

Jean-Marie Charpentier's design fuses classic Chinese culture with contemporary architecture.

ceiling, it functions as a large trumpet, directing the sound from stage to audience. Sound distribution is controlled by the partitions between seating zones, which double as sound-reflection balustrades to narrow the width of the auditorium, and by zigzag boards at the sides of the hall which combine with the three boxes on each side to reflect sound. For opera a curtain is lowered to absorb sound and reduce the reverberation time to 1.3–1.4 seconds; for orchestral performances it is raised to increase the reverberation time to 1.8–1.9 seconds. Sophisticated lighting equipment can produce an infinite number of visual effects.

The complex also contains a theatre seating 600, and a studio theatre seating 200 for performances of chamber music, drama and dance. The extensive support facilities consist of twelve rehearsal rooms of various sizes, practice rooms, dance studios, scenery workshops and dressing rooms to accommodate world-class ballet troupes, opera companies and orchestras.

It is increasingly being recognized that the quality of public space around iconic architecture such as this can be instrumental in public acceptance of the building. Accordingly, Charpentier has designed a flight of stairs leading up between cascading fountains to one of the theatre's entrances. It provides not only an entrance through which to welcome VIPs, but also an arena for the enjoyment of outdoor shows and of the exterior architecture.

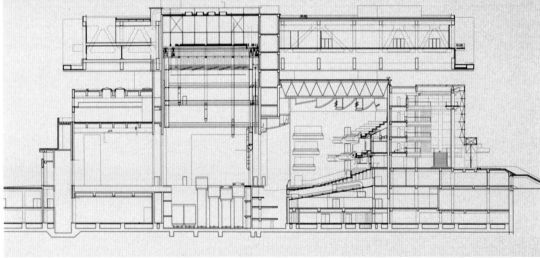

Top left: Glass-encased columns support the roof but allow plenty of light through into the building.

Left: In the longitudinal section, the entrance atrium, with its many levels, is to the right; the huge and very flexible backstage areas to the left.

Opposite: The vast foyer makes extensive use of a rare white marble.

Client
City of Shanghai
Capacity
1800 (auditorium)
600 (drama theatre)
200 (studio theatre)
Area
62,800 sq. m/676,000 sq. ft
Cost
£44.8m/$75m

THE LOWRY PERFORMING AND VISUAL ARTS CENTRE
MICHAEL WILFORD & PARTNERS
SALFORD, UK 2000

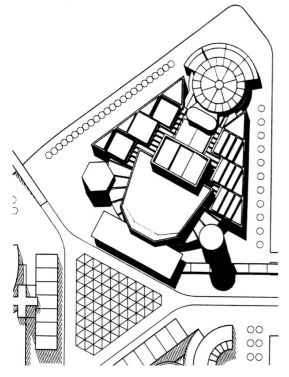

Despite the centre's motley collection of forms (top), its symmetry is evident in plan (above). Two central theatres are flanked by art galleries. A triangular plaza forms the point of entry, and leads to the foyer (opposite), which has a real air of theatricality.

The Lowry Centre is a textbook product of the British government's Millennium Projects programme, funded by the successful National Lottery introduced in 1994, which sought to distribute money to 'good causes', including culture. Despite its many detractors (and many failed projects), the programme has managed to breathe life into a tired industry and to produce many inspirational projects around the UK.

Located on the edge of the 1894 Manchester ship canal in the North of England's former industrial heartland, Salford was not a haven for the arts. Its strongest claim to cultural importance was arguably the painter L.S. Lowry (1887–1976), who lived and worked in Manchester. The Salford Quays area was earmarked for regeneration and the idea of a theatre was first raised in 1988. James Stirling Michael Wilford and Associates were subsequently appointed as masterplanners in 1991. Following the death of James Stirling in 1992, it fell to Michael Wilford to create a home for the city's Lowry collection and to provide a stimulating multi-use venue for education and recreation.

The result is pure 'shrink-wrapped culture', providing something for everyone. As well as the Lowry gallery itself, the centre contains a 1730-seat lyric theatre, a 470-seat flexible theatre, public plaza, hotel, waterfront restaurant, children's gallery and shops. Crucially, the complex is served by a new metro link direct into the centre of Manchester.

Approaching the building from one of three primary routes, the visitor arrives at the public plaza, a gathering point for community activity. Waterside promenades provide pleasant links between the building's entrance and the quays. The centre's two-storey foyer flanks the plaza and is itself a part of the public realm, encouraging casual visitors to enter the building.

The heart of the building is the lyric theatre, all levels of which are served by stairs and balconies from an outer enclosure. Pavilions on either side of the entrance give access to the children's gallery and Lowry gallery above. The shops can be accessed from both foyer and plaza. The flexible theatre is laid out in the form of a courtyard to suit proscenium, traverse, thrust and in-the-round performances.

Wilford has made full use of every opportunity to create exciting viewpoints, whether simply glimpses of other activities and areas, or full panoramas. The internal promenade links all activities, enabling visitors to browse and enjoy the facilities throughout the day; and the curved bar at the end of the quay provides excellent views across the ship canal. The bar, café and restaurant run along the southern side of the building, serving both theatres, and in fine weather they are extended on to quayside terraces overlooking the canal basin used for turning by traditional narrowboats. Upper-level bars on either side of the main theatre open on to roof terraces overlooking the plaza and quaysides.

Mindful of the theatre's hidden side, the backstage area, Wilford has provided well for performers and support staff, aiming to establish a sense of 'artistic community'. To this end, the customary rehearsal rooms are augmented with dedicated areas including an artists' lounge with roof garden. The complex is crowned by a tower housing administration facilities, which has a great impact on the Salford skyline and announces with illuminated signs not only the centre's existence but also forthcoming events. To the uneducated eye the Lowry Centre might look like a hotchpotch of indiscriminate forms, but there is method in Wilford's apparent madness. The appearance of the building is informed by his aim to reflect its many diverse functions in its structure: "The Lowry Centre comprises a unique assembly of forms and spaces which express the range of the building's significance from cultural symbol to intimate place of personal experience."

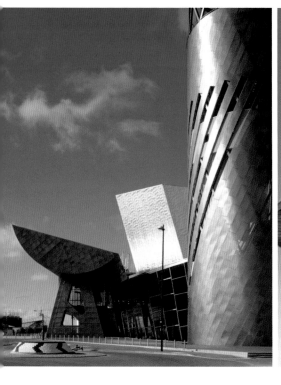  

Above: The focal point is a tall, gleaming tower housing offices (left); the architect has created a stimulating assembly of forms and textures (right), one of which is the curved bar overlooking the canal (centre).

Left: The theatre volume is in the centre, with galleries to either side and the office tower to the right.

Below left: The central spine leads from the plaza and entrance (to the left) to the spectacular canalside bar (to the right).

Right: The creative use of colour and light enhances a range of ancillary spaces.

Pages 36–37: The Lowry has created pleasant and welcoming public space.

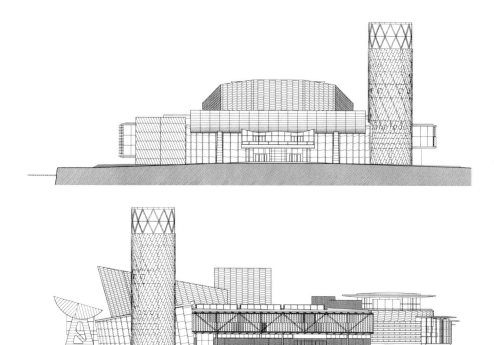

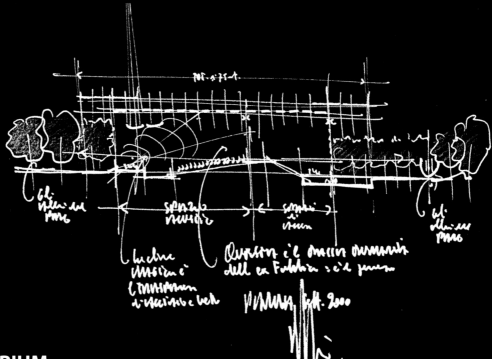

NICCOLÒ PAGANINI AUDITORIUM
RENZO PIANO BUILDING WORKSHOP
PARMA, ITALY 1899/2001

In creating an exciting performance space from a disused sugar factory, Renzo Piano has achieved one of the great aims of today's urban planners: sympathetic regeneration. As the commercial world moves on and the balance shifts from manufacturing towards a new era of technology and services, we are left with a legacy of decaying, unused structures. These derelict megaliths, often unsuitable for today's requirements, are usually consigned to the bulldozer. However, every now and then an excellent architect and the right building come together to provide a stunning new space. Herzog & de Meuron's Tate Modern in London, converted from a power station, is a perfect example. The structure is saved from demolition and its rebirth celebrated, but it retains a connection to its past life.

Close to the medieval heart of Parma and, surprisingly, set in parkland complete with a fine complement of beautiful trees, the 1899 Eridania sugar factory complex consisted of a group of industrial buildings of differing structures and volumes. On assessment, it was found that the main block fitted the basic proportions required for the acoustics of an auditorium. An adjacent building to the east was used to house the service and rehearsal spaces, and the remaining ancillary buildings were demolished.

The exterior envelope of the main building, the 'shoebox', as Piano calls it, was retained, but all internal walls and floors

were removed. Even after the bracing provided by the floors was lost, the longitudinal walls were robust enough to withstand the lateral forces imposed by the iron roof trusses. The two end walls have been replaced with glass screens and a third glazed screen divides the internal space, creating a vast foyer. The result is a vast cathedral-like space 90 m (295 ft) long and three storeys high. The glazed ends frame the views across the parkland, creating a telescope effect that helps to focus the eye on distant objects.

The auditorium runs approximately north–south; the orchestra platform is at the northern end and the public enters from the south. This configuration is deliberate and ensures that a visitor has to experience the full length of the building before arriving at his or her seat, entering first through an impressive covered area that is essentially an extension of the 'telescope' roof and side walls but with an open end. Even here, the height betrays the scale of the hall beyond. From here, the real entrance in the form of the glazed screen both dominates and beckons, and the screen permits tantalizing glimpses of the foyer inside, its two levels connected by a grand staircase. A true showman himself, Piano has ensured that the majesty of his building is revealed in stages. Having arrived in the foyer and climbed to the upper level, the visitor sees the concert hall itself through the next screen. The gently raking seating is arranged so that the lower

Below: Piano has inserted a glass screen into the end wall, creating a dramatic entrance.

Left: The concept sketch shows Piano's concern for transparency and the building's integration with its surroundings.

end is set on the ground-floor level, in an elegant simplicity of design.

In a new building the acoustic requirements can largely be used to generate the form, but here the technical requirements of the auditorium have to be adapted to the existing structure and fabric. New and old meet at every turn, and Piano has proved that with imagination they can be made to work in harmony. Above the orchestra, acoustic panels formed of curved wood hang from the original roof trusses while the lines of the building's previous three floors are revealed in the rectangular fenestration which the architect has left in the flank walls. The walls themselves have been treated with acoustic plaster.

A range of lighting effects is achieved by varying combinations of artificial and natural lighting. The sheer number of side windows provides a multitude of variations, with a system of blinds controlling the natural light. Under certain conditions the highest windows can cast shafts of light, adding to the cathedral atmosphere.

The Eridania sugar factory was conceived as a dynamic production machine, an important part of the local community, but the vital commercial oxygen had long ceased to flow, and the building was all but dead. Renzo Piano's vision has breathed new life into the structure, and has brought the building once more into the heart of the community.

Top: The shallow entrance stairs lead to the top of the gently raked seating.

Above: Stripped of its original floors, the new space is flooded with light through its many windows.

Right: The impressive entrance. The foyer is behind the first glazed wall.

Opposite: The original fenestration is retained, showing clearly the building's former configuration.

Client
Comune di Parma.
Capacity
780
Area
Not available
Cost
£8.4m/$11.9m/ €13.9m

KIMMEL CENTER FOR THE PERFORMING ARTS
RAFAEL VIÑOLY ARCHITECTS
PHILADELPHIA, USA 2001

The bold yet sympathetic architecture of Philadelphia's new landmark, strategically placed on the Avenue of the Arts, is striking. Its soaring, glazed barrel-vaulted roof is an elegant solution to the problem of connecting the city's high-rise and low-rise districts. The issue of 'delineation', and how its impact can be decreased, is clearly one of Viñoly's passions, and he has shown with this project how iconic architecture can be successfully fused into an existing streetscape.

The Kimmel Center is a new home for the Philadelphia Orchestra, which, since its foundation in 1900, had occupied the 1857 Academy of Music. Although popular with locals, the building was dogged by poor acoustics inherent in the structure, and for decades the management had been striving to build a new facility.

As well as the zoning restrictions, Viñoly had to overcome another hurdle, that of avoiding the sense of élitism associated with buildings for the performing arts. He has sought to create a building that is more accessible and acceptable to the community. This has largely been achieved by imaginative (and exhaustive) attention to the building's boundary with the street. Viñoly explains the concept: "The fabric of the city flows into the heart of the complex, Commonwealth Plaza, effectively creating a sheltered extension of the sidewalk outside and blurring the distinction between the city and the Center. Here cafés, free performances including puppet shows, the spectacle of the space, and the people who come to see it and share it combine to create an exciting civic experience for concert-goers, tourists, commuters and musicians alike."

Viñoly likens the building's two principal components, the Verizon Hall and the Perelman Theater, to "two jewels in a glass case". The venues are treated as freestanding buildings. Verizon Hall, with its polygonal makore wood exterior, is positioned at the centre of one end of the site. The Perelman Theater, with its curved façade in black granite and its main volume clad in metal, is placed off the main axis toward the front of the site. Enclosing both structures is a perimeter building constructed from brick, steel and concrete,

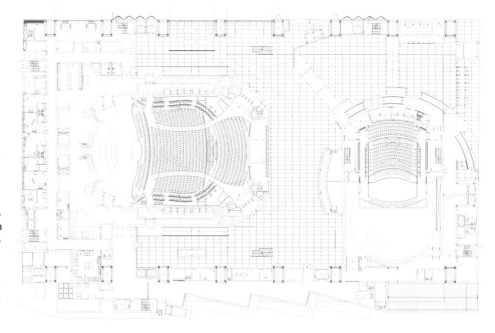

and the space between and around them becomes an enormous indoor area, Commonwealth Plaza. Arching over all the structures is the vast vaulted roof of folded steel and glass creating a spectacular indoor–outdoor experience. The glazed screens closing both ends of the barrel vault presented some engineering challenges. A sophisticated gravity-tensioned cable suspension system supports the 1,000 sq. m (10,750 sq. ft) of museum-quality, very clear glass at each end, the centre points of which can withstand wind-induced deflection of +/- 1 m (3 ft).

Viñoly acknowledges that in order to exorcise the ghosts of the past, acoustics were fundamental to the project. The Verizon Hall was thus created first as a musical instrument, and second as a piece of architecture. Formed in the shape of a cello and clad in mahogany with no orthogonal surfaces, the interior was designed in accordance with the principles of ideal sound production. The orchestra, the source of the sound, is at a location equivalent to the position of the cello's bridge, a confluence of energy connecting the strings to the sounding body of the instrument. The inherent properties of architectural form are usually insufficient in their own right to create the desired range of acoustic options, and this design was no exception. The internal walls are formed entirely of one hundred doors at different levels; they can be opened to allow sound to escape into vast reverberation chambers in the void between these walls and those of the building itself. Depending on the doors' configuration, reverberation time can be lengthened by increasing the hall's volume by as much as thirty per cent. Augmenting this is a battery of retractable sound-absorbing curtains and an acoustic canopy that can be configured to direct sound out into the audience while allowing the musicians to hear themselves clearly.

This much sought-after acoustic perfection initially proved elusive, however, and early performances attracted mixed press reviews, including an infamous comment in the *Washington Post* likening the Verizon Hall to an "acoustical Sahara". This must in part have been caused by the complexities of fine-tuning the cello-shaped hall, with the number of acoustic variations increased exponentially by the number of acoustic doors opened.

The brief for the Perelman Hall was to provide a multi-functional facility accommodating an audience of 650 for theatre, music and dance performances. Two key features aid flexibility: the first is a turntable stage, which enables the theatre to be transformed from a conventional proscenium configuration into a smaller arena with concert shell and wraparound seating; secondly, the entire parquet seating section is supported by hydraulic risers that enable the pitch of the floor to be adjusted or even flattened to create a ballroom or banqueting hall.

On the roof, a stunning garden gives impressive views of the city over the remainder of the complex.

Above: A dramatic, light and airy space has been created on top of the Perelman Theater.

Opposite: The Kimmel's glass envelope encases a multitude of shapes and forms. The Verizon Theater is the wooden volume, and the granite and metal Perelman Theater is in front.

Pages 46–47: The timeless red plush of the cello-shaped Verizon Hall disguises a modern and fully flexible acoustic profile.

Client
Regional Performing Arts Center
Capacity
2500 (Verizon Theater)
650 (Perelman Theater)
Area
42,400 sq. m/460,000 sq. ft
Cost
£187m/$265m/€310m

NEW TEMPODROM
VON GERKAN, MARG & PARTNER
BERLIN, GERMANY 2001

Below right: The main arena's plan is perfectly circular, and bars are arranged around its outer walls. The smaller auditorium is at top right, and the Liquidrom at bottom right.

Bottom and opposite: The Tempodrom is set high up for impact. An imposing flight of stairs leads to the terrace.

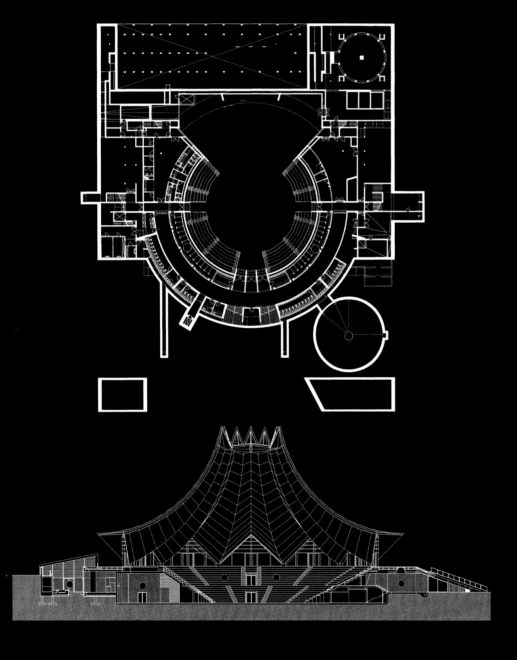

The Tempodrom has its cultural roots firmly in Berlin. Founded in 1980 by a nurse, Irene Moessinger, and a group of her friends, it presented many varied events inside two 'big tops' that proved a big success with Berliners, attracting some 200,000 visitors each season. Over the following twenty years it had a somewhat nomadic existence, being located first at Potsdamer Place next to the Berlin Wall, then at Tiergarten and later at Ostbahnhof.

It has now been recreated as a permanent building. Its heritage is clear, but the use of technology, materials and elegant contemporary design is symbolic of modern Germany; and in this way its rebirth closely resembles that of the Volkswagen 'Beetle'. This regeneration of an established design is something the Germans have clearly mastered to perfection. It is also fitting that what must be the world's only theatre building in the form of a tensile structure should be located in Germany, home of the great pioneer of that technology, Frei Otto (born 1925). However, one of this building's many surprises is that the roof is in fact constructed from steel and concrete. It bears a striking resemblance to Oscar Niemeyer's cathedral in Brasilia, also a stark white beacon of new hope and part of the plan for a new city.

The site of the building, on the former Anhalter Bahnhof train terminus (once known as the 'gateway to the south'), provided an opportunity for urban regeneration and the creation of a new public space. This was one of the planning team's key objectives. The complex consists of three venues: the main arena, with 3800 seats; the smaller arena, with 400 seats; and the Liquidrom, a pool 13 m (43 ft) in diameter set in a domed concrete shell, with underwater speakers, where fifty visitors can lie in lukewarm salt water and experience a light and sound show. A strong connection between the theatre and the public piazza is created by a wide flight of steps to the north leading up to the entrance, and a roof terrace that serves as a beer garden in summer.

The dominant feature of the new Tempodrom is its dramatic, sweeping roof rising some 37 m (121 ft) above the piazza. Formed of a load-bearing steel framework clad with pre-cast concrete panels 120 cm (47 in.) thick, it bears down on to twelve cylindrical steel supports, which are in turn supported by a conventional foundation structure. Such great roof mass is needed because of the acoustic challenges posed by pop concerts, which can generate as much as 100 decibels.

Despite its futuristic appearance, the theatre deliberately takes on a more conservative approach inside, with most

walls and ceilings being finished in fair-faced concrete. However, the architects have used the inherent form of the structure to allow in natural light. Peripheral fenestration takes the form of triangular glazing that naturally fills the gaps created by the segmented roof eaves. The origami-like apex also houses cleverly concealed glazing invisible from the outside.

The architects have created all-important flexibility wherever possible. The front five rows of seats in the main hall are detachable, so that the performing space can be extended by 9 m (30 ft). The secondary space with its concentric seating steps is open to the foyer, but can be turned into an intimate event hall with moveable partition walls. Ancillary functions for some 150 people are provided by four lecture rooms, and the complex has a 70-seat restaurant.

The Tempodrom, although an unusual structure, is clearly a great success, paying homage to its origins but also taking the theatre into the twenty-first century.

Opposite: The roof sweeps upwards from above the triangular windows.

Right: Cleverly concealed glazing at the apex of the 'tent' allows light to penetrate.

Below right: The Liquidrom is a quiet, cool space finished in smooth concrete.

Client
Stiftung Neues
Tempodrom
Capacity
3800 (main arena)
400 (smaller arena)
50 (Liquidrom)
Area
12,400 sq. m/130,000 sq. ft
Cost
£18m/$25.6m/€30m

ARCIMBOLDI OPERA THEATRE
GREGOTTI ASSOCIATI INTERNATIONAL
MILAN, ITALY 2002

A new opera house in Milan, the centre of the opera world, is always going to be of significant interest. Taking its place beside La Scala as the second grand opera theatre in Milan – although it is actually the largest – the Arcimboldi's first task was to stand in for the premier theatre during its refurbishment in 2002–4. The strength of the link between La Scala and the Arcimboldi is indicated by the fact that the same stage sets were used in both theatres. To accommodate this, the stage of the Arcimboldi was created with similar dimensions to that of La Scala, and the proscenium fixed at 16 m (52 ft) wide and 12 m (39 ft) high. The programme of the Arcimboldi is predominantly classical and opera, but it also accommodates other events.

The Arcimboldi was officially opened on 19 January 2002 with Verdi's *La Traviata* conducted by Riccardo Muti, La Scala's musical director. Its glory was shortlived, however, as it had to be closed for a few days later that month when glass panels crashed on to empty seats during a performance. The audience was safely evacuated from the auditorium after creaking noises were heard, and two of the acoustic panels lining the walls fell 6 m (20 ft) to the floor. The incident overshadowed the debut of the building, already the subject of controversy over the speed with which it had been built, in just twenty-seven months.

The new theatre, sponsored by Italian tyre firm Pirelli, has been created to meet the high demand for musical concerts and performances in the Milanese metropolitan area. It is to serve the vast catchment area of northern Italy (with a population of more than three million people from Sesto San Giovanni and Monza to Lecco, Como and Varese), as well as the city of Milan, and is suitably situated in Bicocca where it is served directly by both rail and motorways.

It must be said that given the expectations for the building, and Milan's reputation for design, flair and style, the exterior of the Arcimboldi is somewhat disappointing. The rectilinear form with its massive 'windscreen' resembles that of a car, or on this scale a large truck. The outside walls are finished in white plaster with a black granite base, and the building opens on to a large square to which the main routes from the large public car park and the metro-tram and train stations lead. Vittorio Gregotti explains that "in the context of the entire area, the building functions as an authentic landmark: it is detached from the surrounding regular urban plan so as to return to the organization of the area's pre-industrial development."

Perhaps the real value of this building is its technical performance, and inside the shell, this is where the focus has been directed. The architect has employed the most advanced technical solutions for acoustic quality and stage design. The stage tower measures 32 × 27 m (105 × 89 ft), and is 40 m (131 ft) high; the theatre holds an audience of 2375 divided into interconnected stalls on two levels, and two circles. The walls of the large hall are finished in red-painted wood, while the plaster ceiling has a complex articulation designed to achieve the best acoustic quality. The ill-fated adjustable glass side panels, one hundred in total, function as both sound deflectors and lighting screens for the hall.

The theatre structure houses all the necessary ancillary services, including offices, dressing rooms, a double rehearsal room, and restaurants and bars. The reception, cloakroom, bookshop, café, services and entrance foyers are housed in an area 15 m (50 ft) high that is ordered by the columns bearing the inclined fully-glazed 'windscreen'. On the northern side of the square, a building with a pillared portico houses the ticket office and a restaurant.

Now that La Scala has reopened, it will be interesting to observe the future of the new building; presumably the Arcimboldi's strength will be its ability to accommodate a greater range of events than the older house. Its prosaic appearance notwithstanding, it is a valuable and well thought-out building in which real attention has been paid to technical performance, arguably the over-ruling aspect of any performing-arts space.

Below left: The auditorium makes bold use of colour.

Bottom left: The foyer is a warm and inviting space.

Opposite top: At night-time the building is dominated by light radiating from the vast glazed roof.

Opposite bottom: The new theatre nestles in its industrial surroundings.

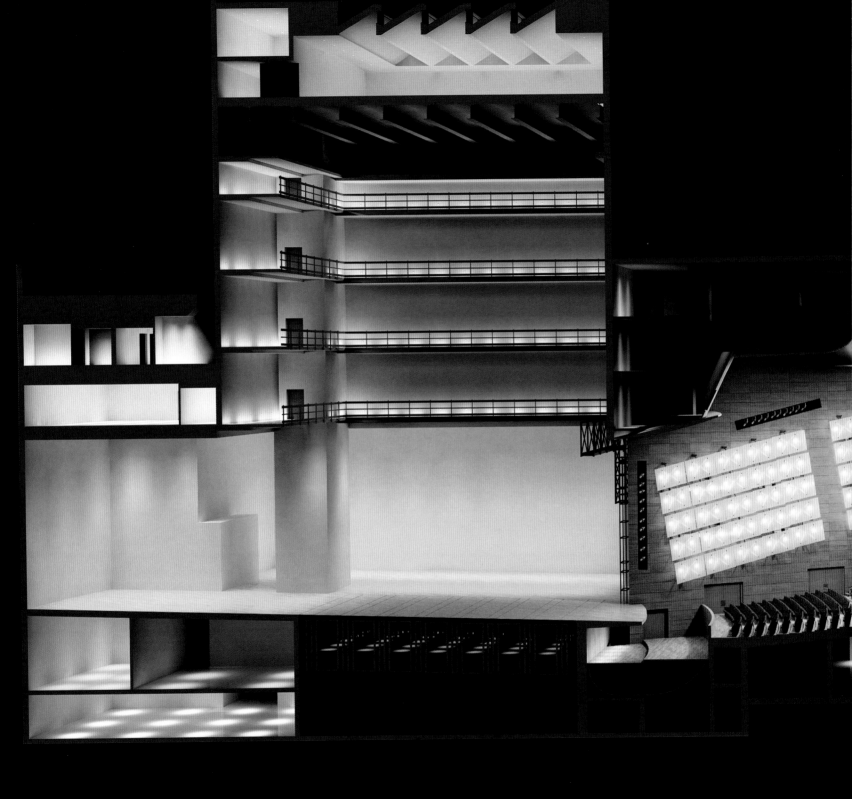

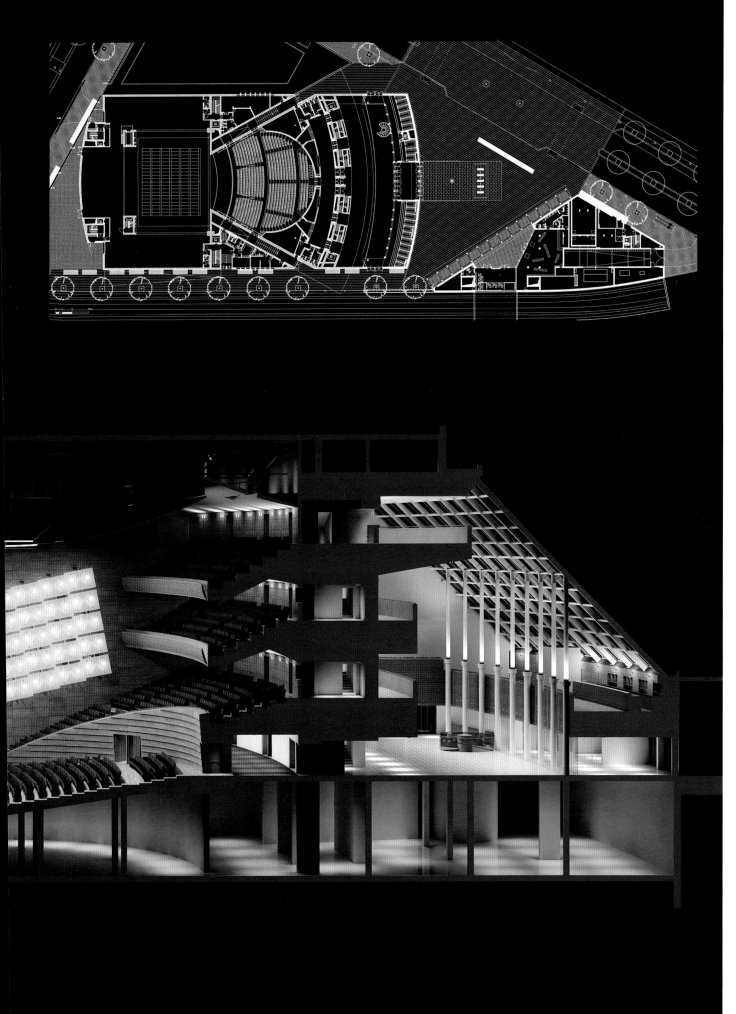

Left: The Arcimboldi
sits comfortably on an
awkwardly shaped site.
The restaurant and ticket
office are in the separate
volume at bottom right.

Below left: The glass
screens fixed to the walls
are for both acoustics
and lighting.

Client
Milan City Council
Capacity
2375
Area
7400 sq. m/80,000 sq. ft
Cost
£28.5m/$42.7m/€44m

AUDITORIUM PARCO DELLA MUSICA
RENZO PIANO BUILDING WORKSHOP
ROME, ITALY 2002

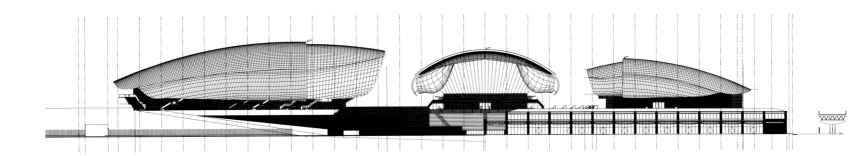

Opposite: Piano's design encases the music venues in metal-clad shells.

Above: The three covered performing spaces face each other across the outdoor arena.

Conceived by Renzo Piano as a city of music, Parco della Musica is unusually focused for a contemporary performing-arts project. Not here the multi-functional requirements of theatre, ballet and concerts – just music of all kinds. With one outdoor and three enclosed performing spaces, giving the complex a total capacity of 7700, this is the largest concert hall in Europe. There are no constraints such as those imposed by the pre-existing envelope of the Niccolò Paganini Auditorium (see pp. 38–41), and so Piano could be more expressive, beginning the design with a clean sheet.

Enriching Rome's vast cultural heritage was not going to be an easy task, but the sheer scale and ambition of this complex show the city's determination to make an impact. The site, described by Piano as 'decentralized', is well serviced by the transport infrastructure already in place for the nearby 1960 Olympic Village, Pier Luigi Nervi's Palazzetto dello Sport and the Flaminio Stadium. Piano sees the site as an "artificial fracture" in the fabric of the city and his design as a "healing" element in the urban tissue.

Almost as soon as the project started on site, work was halted by the discovery of a villa dating from the fourth century. A not uncommon occurrence in Rome, the discovery of archaeological remains triggered a well-orchestrated response, and the layout of the site was modified to include a museum of the Roman remains.

Piano admits that "all the spaces have been conceived with music in mind". One cannot help wondering whether he was so focused on the performance aspects that his external treatment of the structures suffered, resulting in what could be described as a group of titanic 'orchestral hangars'. The volumes needed to achieve the required acoustics result in a vast surface area with a battleship-like finish, and the lack of any fenestration simply amplifies the effect. As for the interiors, Piano explains: "Each of the three concert halls is conceived as a virtual musical instrument, has its individual characteristics and is the fruit of previous experience gained in the domain of acoustics. These huge 'musical boxes' are structurally as well as architecturally and functionally separate, to facilitate soundproofing. Each one is equipped for sound recording."

The 2800-seat concert hall can accommodate a large orchestra and choir for symphonic works. The central stage, with its modular configuration, guarantees perfect visibility and sound quality. The volume of this hall is at the maximum for effective natural acoustics. Its layout, like those of many of the greatest concert halls, is based on a *vignetto* design, echoing the terracing of vineyards.

A key factor in the design of the 1200-seat concert hall is flexibility. The stage and seating can be adjusted according to the performance's requirements, allowing

fine-tuning of the reverberation time. This flexibility permits a range of performance types, from large orchestral concerts with choir, to contemporary music.

The 700-seat concert hall has a traditional orchestra pit and fly tower. The three planes (two lateral and one vertical) that form the stage can be opened out, allowing its size to be increased or decreased. The hall can house operas, chamber music and baroque performances, as well as symphonic concerts.

In accordance with the complex's main purpose, the rehearsal rooms (whether they be for the use of a symphony orchestra or a soloist), foyer and open-air amphitheatre are all devoted to music. Of the two main rehearsal rooms, one is dedicated to choirs and the other, being more flexible, can accommodate a choir and a large orchestra. These rooms allow the musicians to practise in the best acoustic conditions, and can also serve as recording studios. By employing mobile elements and acoustic curtains, the reverberation time can be adjusted to the music's requirements.

The complex also contains a museum of musical instruments, offices and a specialist library.

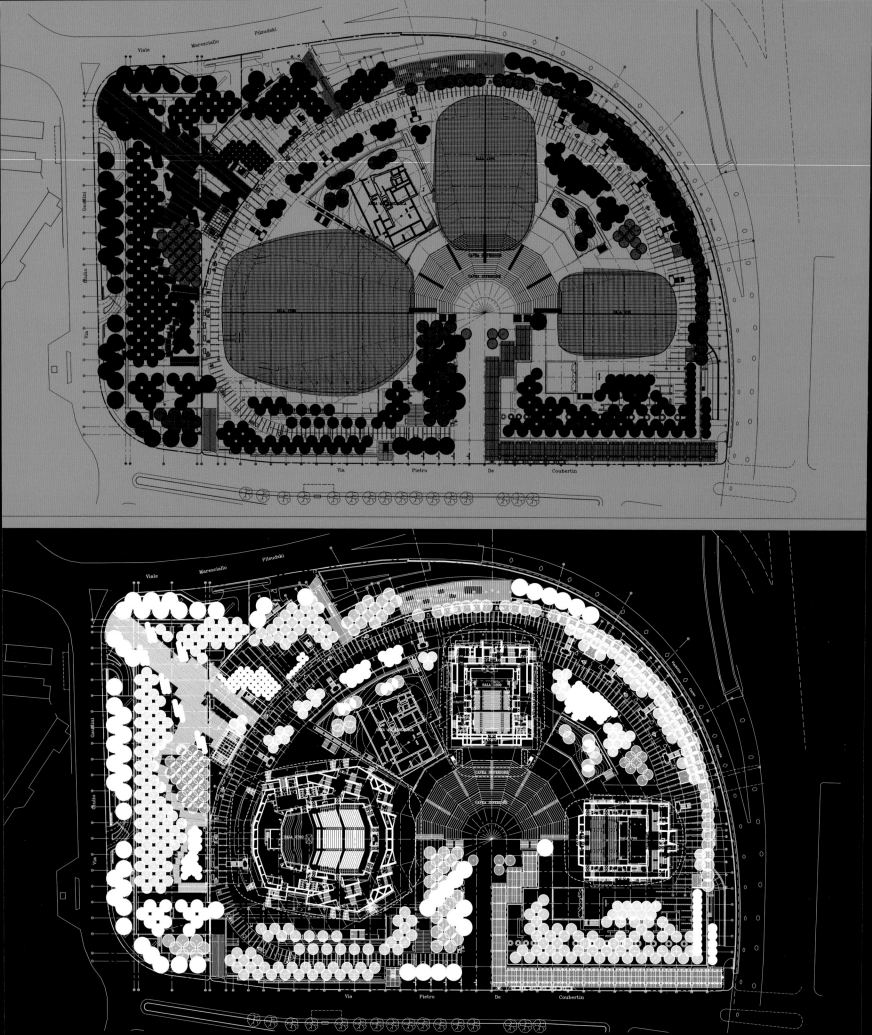

Opposite: Site plans
show the auditoria
covered (top) and
uncovered (bottom).

Right: The large hangar-
like spaces have no
windows, and structural
elements are highly
visible, increasing the
strictly utilitarian feel
of the complex.

Client
City of Rome
Capacity
2800; 1200; 700 (halls)
3000 (outdoor arena)
Area
55,000 sq. m/600,000 sq. ft
Cost
£94m/$140.7m/€145.2m

Originally built in 1804 as a stable block for the Prince Regent, the Brighton Dome is now a Grade I-listed concert hall and, with six hundred performances each year, arguably the hub of the town's vibrant performing-arts scene. The original design was modelled on the Corn Exchange in Paris, which was designed in the 'Hindu' style highly fashionable at the time. The Dome was not used as a concert hall until 1867, but it soon became the most popular and culturally significant venue in the south of England. Following its restoration in 1935, complete with outstanding Art Deco interior, it showcased some of the world's biggest names in entertainment. The building has just emerged from a refit under the direction of London-based architects Arts Team, and now forms a complex consisting of a concert hall, the Pavilion Theatre, the Corn Exchange (a flexible performing-arts and multi-use space) and a museum.

The project was an immense challenge for Arts Team, and took fifteen years to

realize. The building's fabric was in severe disrepair, and the theatre would have been forced to close had a National Lottery grant not come to the rescue. The brief asked for a world-class, adaptable concert hall, because it was thought unlikely that sufficient funding or audiences could be found to support a hall purely for classical music. Constraints were everywhere: not only was the original 1804 building envelope listed but also the 1935 Art Deco interior. The architects had to deal with the building's dreadful acoustics – caused by the small volume of the auditorium and the thin 1930s ceiling – and with the problem of heat build-up caused by the glass roof.

An array of air handling, mechanical, electrical and acoustic services had to be accommodated without affecting either the listed interior or the earlier exterior. This was to be one of the most taxing aspects for the team. Compounding this problem, the theatre had been in use until the moment the building works began, preventing an exhaustive survey. This

BRIGHTON DOME CONCERT HALL
ARTS TEAM
BRIGHTON, UK 2002

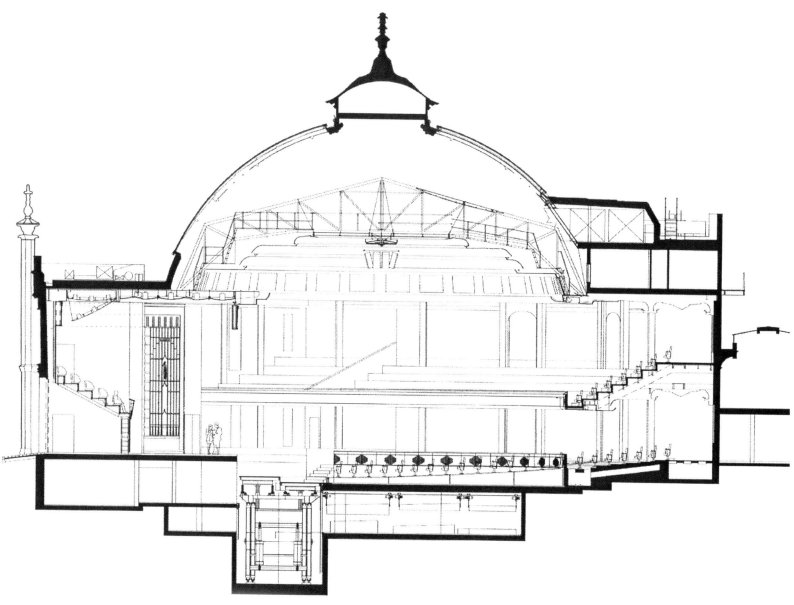

situation inevitably led to some unforeseen problems, one of which was the condition of the interior fabric. The entire dome had to be strengthened and its support structure replaced. Eventually, after ingress of water during construction, parts of the interior were replaced. At the same time, the team inserted many of the services, including the bulky air-handling ducts, between the 1930s ceiling and the original domed roof.

The target reverberation time of 1.8 seconds, the ideal for orchestral performances, was achieved in two steps. The first stage was to increase the mass of the concert hall envelope. The Art Deco ceiling was replaced with layers of medium-density fibreboard and large reflective panels were installed on the perimeter walls.

The second stage was to install an electronic enhancement system. Acoustic engineers Arup were responsible for fulfilling this aspect of the brief. After trials of various products, a new French system called 'Carmen' was chosen. It was the first time this system had been used in the UK, but the likely benefits were thought to be so great as to outweigh the risk. The Carmen system uses a fundamentally different approach to that of conventional systems. Traditionally, microphones placed above the orchestra take sample sounds; these are enhanced and then broadcast around the auditorium with loudspeakers, each of which delivers an identical sound. The Carmen system operates on a cell principle, taking samples from all around the auditorium. The sound is processed locally and introduced back to the hall through individual loudspeakers. The effect is remarkable: transparent and very natural. The acoustics have been a tremendous success, winning accolades from all quarters, in particular the performers.

Other events, such as rock concerts, require a reverberation time nearer to one second. To accommodate this, the wall panels are reversible, with a sound-absorbent surface on the back. They can be 'flipped' very quickly using a simple hinged mechanism reminiscent of the secret revolving panels seen in old movies.

On the Dome's reopening, after two and a half years of construction and some £17m of costs, many patrons exclaimed, "You haven't done anything!" Considering that the entire interior had been replaced, this was praise indeed.

Opposite: The architects moved the services into the generous space between the ceiling and the dome.

Left: The early nineteenth-century façades on Church Street are unbroken, despite the high level of modernization carried out on the Dome's structure.

Below: The architects have incorporated a modern bar area, complete with mezzanine.

Opposite left and right: The internal finishes have been completely replaced.

Opposite bottom: In its newly refurbished state, the concert hall is once again a popular part of Brighton's cultural life.

Right and below: Despite its traditional appearance, the auditorium has such high-tech acoustic features as revolving wall panels. It is crowned by an elegant 1930s-style ceiling.

Client
Brighton Festival Society
Capacity
1878
Area
Not available
Cost
£17.4m/$26m/€27m

Left: From the water, the building is resplendent, its fish-like exterior glowing with the light from inside.

Below: The floor plan shows the logical arrangement of spaces underneath the enclosing skin.

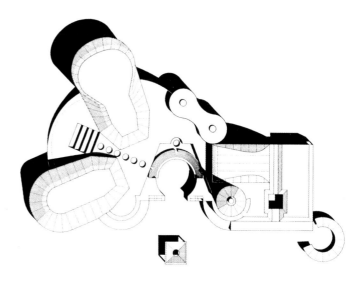

ESPLANADE NATIONAL PERFORMING ARTS CENTRE
MICHAEL WILFORD & PARTNERS
SINGAPORE 2002

Through progressive reclamation of land, Singapore's city centre had lost its focal relationship with water. Michael Wilford's aim for the new arts centre was to 'reconnect' the city to the sea (as now represented by Marina Bay). Other factors were to emerge, however, that would influence the design process and outcome.

Wilford is openly critical of many contemporary schemes: "Much recent architecture fails to respond to the rich cultural diversity arising out of its geographic location and history. In addition to expressing technology and responding to climate, architecture needs to re-establish cultural continuity with the past in order to hypothesize about the future." He wanted to prove that it was possible to "express the fusion between modern technology and local traditions".

As well as noting practicalities such as the locations of entrances, the brief specified that the concourse should form the focus of the building, overlooking Marina Bay, and be centred on the intersection of the urban axes generated by Fort Canning and Marina Square. It asked that the centre have a clear iconic image,

but that intrusion into Marina Park be minimized by sensitive landscaping.

Despite Wilford's sensitivity to the building's context, his early designs were criticized as being "too Western". He therefore took the unusual step in 1996 of holding a competition in which a number of consultant teams were invited to develop façade solutions to enclose the scheme, which by this time had been otherwise resolved.

The winners were Atelier One and its sister company Atelier Ten, who beat such established contenders as Arup Façade Engineering. Their innovative proposal returned to first principles, studying the basic functions of a skin from those of indigenous buildings to animals. This approach led them to identify the skin's primary function as one of temperature regulation. Developing their design from this principle, their aim was to "produce a skin that would draw on passive environmental techniques to create a buffer zone, or bio-climatic environment, that would moderate the climate between the fully conditioned and sealed environments of the two major black-box

performance spaces and the ever-changing external environment".

The challenge to get the balance of architecture, climate, structure and economy correct for the two 8000 sq. m (86,000 sq. ft) areas was significant. The engineers used a sophisticated 'inflation' modelling technique to produce a structure supported by struts of equal size – a great aid to manufacturing and installation.

The final envelope is formed of a tubular-steel frame filled with diamond-shaped, double-glazed, insulated aluminium panels. Added to these were the striking aluminium shading cowls that vary in angle according to their position: flat on the horizontal surfaces (minimizing direct sunlight), they take on a 'beak' appearance on the vertical surfaces (reducing low incident light). These environmental devices in the envelope design had a direct impact on the building's appearance: the modulated skin took on the combined qualities of the scales and gills of a fish. This reference to the harbour was well received by the client.

Inside, the building bustles with activity, with its three theatres, studio and concert hall. The hall is used for symphonic, choral, Asian and popular music as well as conventions, broadcasting and recording. Between them, the theatres accommodate musicals, Chinese and Western opera, traditional dance, ballet, popular and chamber music, jazz, modern dance and all types of drama as well as television performances, lectures and multimedia events.

For many, the real magic of this building is the dramatic sense of place in the 'leftover' spaces between the theatres and the enclosure. The curvaceous shapes of these public areas are the by-products of two separate design processes – those of the acoustic- and logistic-driven performing zones, and the climatic- and structure-driven envelope. The windows of these spaces are flanked by sweeping balconies and framed by vast alien-like structures of steel, affording fantastic glimpses of the city and other parts of the complex.

Opposite top: Close up, the intriguing façade reveals itself as an arrangement of glazing and aluminium cowls.

Opposite bottom: The space between the building's 'skin' and its internal structures creates exciting viewing areas.

Above: The hulking shape of the centre is echoed in the enormous auditorium with its many tiers of seating.

Client
Singapore Public Works Department and Singapore Arts Centre Company Ltd

Capacity
1800 (concert hall)
2000 (lyric theatre)
850 (medium theatre)
450 (adaptable theatre)
250 (development studio)

Area
80,500 sq. m/870,000 sq. ft

Cost
£360m/$540m/€ 557m

PERFORMING ARTS CENTER
BARD COLLEGE OF PERFORMING ARTS
GEHRY PARTNERS

ANNANDALE-ON-HUDSON, NEW YORK, USA 2003

The shimmering stainless steel structure is classic Gehry, but unlike his Guggenheim Museum in Bilbao, its soaring metal planes are largely decorative.

The hilly scenery of the Hudson Valley is a surprising place in which to stumble across a little piece of Bilbao, hidden in a fold. There is none of the international clamour of the Guggenheim Museum, but in the Performing Arts Center of Bard College Gehry has also established the unassuming rural community of Annandale-on-Hudson on the architectural map.

Backed by mountain views and surrounded by trees, the building has been likened to something out of *Hansel and Gretel*. Bard College's original plans were to extend an existing building, but the final stand-alone version has allowed the architect the freedom to create in splendid isolation. The classic Gehry envelope houses teaching, rehearsal and performance rooms for Bard's dance and theatre departments, and provides a home for the American Symphony Orchestra. Its two main spaces are the Sosnoff Theater, a multi-purpose venue that seats 800–900; and the Resnick Theater, a flexible 200-seat teaching and studio theatre.

The brief for the Sosnoff Theater was to create a flexible space that could cater for a diverse performance programme, and that would appear different depending on whether it was in concert mode or dance/theatre mode. Gehry engaged the help of theatre design company Theatre Projects Consultants for the specialist elements. To address the brief's requirements, the proscenium was made flexible and can be retracted sideways and upwards. Douglas fir wood has been used extensively on the theatre walls, and extends on to the stage for concerts in the form of thirteen enormous moveable

telescopic towers wrapping around the stage and three prominent adjustable panels hovering overhead. The result has been well received and, as stipulated in the brief, the theatre looks entirely different in each of its two guises.

Despite the sweeping strokes of the exterior, the centre has obviously been designed with great attention to detail. The seats in the Sosnoff Theater are by Poltrona Frau (the Italian company that makes seats for Ferrari cars), and are made of the same wood as the auditorium; gold thread in their blue upholstery spells out the names of all graduates from the college in 2003. Two balconies each have four side boxes with chairs and higher stools, while benches in the balconies offer maximum capacity for student gatherings.

As always in such spaces, the configuration is something of a trade-off. The theatre's seating is steeply raked and the floors are set far apart, which is good for sightlines; but the shape of the room is dependent on many factors. The hall design and concert tower system define the acoustic quality of the hall, and there are fewer adjustable options than in many other contemporary concert halls. Despite the large volume required to seat 900 people, this hall has been praised for its intimate feel and for the close relationship between the stage and the audience; and it has even been described by the *New Yorker* as "what may be the best small concert hall in the United States".

The brief for the Resnick Theater specified a fully flexible space for dance and drama, but not music. The result fulfils this demand with its moveable seating, yet it

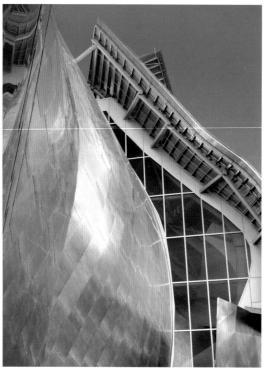

has a fixed end stage and stage house. Because of budget and height restrictions, the stage house is not full height, but it does have a grid. The venue can be used in numerous configurations, from a flat floor to a raked room for end-stage productions, and this flexibility is ideal for experimentation. In contrast to the light and airy atmosphere of the Sosnoff Theater, the Resnick is finished in dark-stained wood.

The building is not pure Guggenheim, as the budget was necessarily smaller; nowhere is this fact more apparent than at the back, where the swirling stainless steel fades to a rudimentary box. The foyer is also basic, with concrete floors and exposed ductwork. Despite these limitations, the building has turned out to be a place of pilgrimage for those interested in architecture: according to John Tissot of Theatre Projects Consultants, "even a year before the opening there were numerous drive-bys". This hidden gem in an idyllic setting certainly shows that it is not necessary to go all the way to Bilbao to see an excellent example of a sculptural Gehry building.

Above: Inside and outside, various structural elements support Gehry's free-form envelope.

Opposite: The cool simplicity of the Sosnoff Theater belies its great adaptability.

Client
Bard College of Performing Arts

Capacity
900 (Sosnoff Theater)
200 (Resnick Theater)

Area
10,200 sq. m/110,000 sq. ft

Cost
£37m/$62m/€53m

TENERIFE AUDITORIUM
SANTIAGO CALATRAVA
SANTA CRUZ DE TENERIFE, SPAIN 2003

On an outcrop of land between the grinding ring roads of Santa Cruz, an industrial container port and the wild Atlantic Ocean, Tenerife's new auditorium takes advantage of a dramatic site. Classic Calatrava in design, the building resembles a giant sea bird trapped by the encroaching, seething mass of city and industrial complexes.

Rising up from the harbour, Santa Cruz itself is encircled by the Anaga Hills. This natural topography combines with the city's high-rise blocks to create a spectacular backdrop for the new auditorium. The visual impact of such a building in Tenerife's capital cannot be overstated. Glimpses of it are revealed at every turn in the city's streets and from the roads feeding in from the surrounding hills,

and its gleaming white surfaces and graceful form draw in the eye. The Tenerife Auditorium is making a statement; the city has established a powerful cultural link through architecture, and the juxtaposition of such a dramatic building with the ocean, mountains and city, like the site of an ancient amphitheatre, has a powerful and exciting effect.

The gleaming exterior walls are constructed from white concrete cast in situ, and finished with broken ceramic tiles (much used in the surrounding area) and granite basalt, creating an unusual sheen. The auditorium's series of structural elements is centred on the conical concert hall. Two outer casings sweep around the auditorium, creating a perimeter space,

which serves as a foyer and as a barrier
from the machinations of the city outside.
Concrete arches support glazed entrances
on either side of the auditorium, the glass
providing a contrast with the rest of the
building. The arches also transfer the loads
from the outer casings to the foundations.
The overriding visual feature is the roof
'wing', which soars to a point 98 m (320 ft)
above the base of its arc. Looking like the
gnomon of a giant sundial, the wing points
north-east over the public plaza and out
across the Atlantic Ocean towards Africa.

Before the visitor arrives at the concert
hall itself, Calatrava delights with a range of
sculptural, curving spaces, from eye-shaped
passageways flanked by glazed galleries
offering commanding views of the Atlantic,

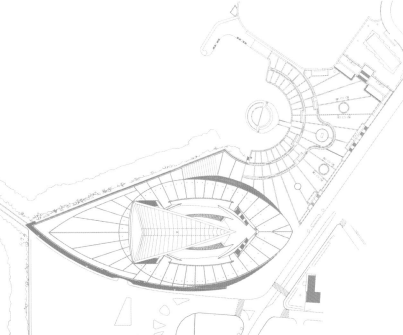

Above: The auditorium
perches like a huge white
bird on its waterside site.

Left: As well as such
radical elements as the
triangular chamber-
music hall, the plan
includes many irregularly
shaped circulation areas
and public spaces.

to twisting and turning flights of stairs like those of a Moorish 'Kasbah'. The fenestration is sometimes open and sometimes glazed.

The Tenerife Auditorium is home to the Tenerife Symphony Orchestra and comprises two main performing areas: a 1660-seat concert hall and a 428-seat hall for chamber music. Calatrava explains that "the curved geometry of the concert hall is the generating element of both the form and structure of the building". The concert hall's radical conical roof creates a unique acoustic characteristic. A series of convex forms reflect the sound, and the acoustic conditions are varied by the regulation of sound-absorbent surfaces behind a rectangular grid.

The hall for chamber music has a triangular footprint of 411 sq. m (4425 sq. ft), and a false ceiling with a dramatic 'palm-leaf' finish. Self-contained, with all the usual amenities – foyer, bar and cloakrooms – it is accessed through a passageway from the main foyer. Finally, a public plaza brings the auditorium to the wider community and, with its magnificent sense of place, has proved to be a popular destination for tourists and locals alike. On the ocean side of the complex, a terrace café provides stunning views.

Calatrava's buildings and structures are all different, but each carries his signature. This building, the forerunner to a bigger version in the architect's home city, Valencia (pp. 120–23), will always be a favourite for visitors because of its location.

The pointed sculptural wing arches over the unusual conical roof of the main concert hall and the public plaza that surrounds the building.

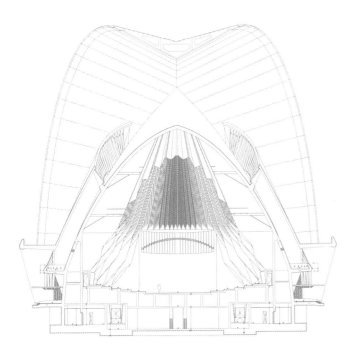

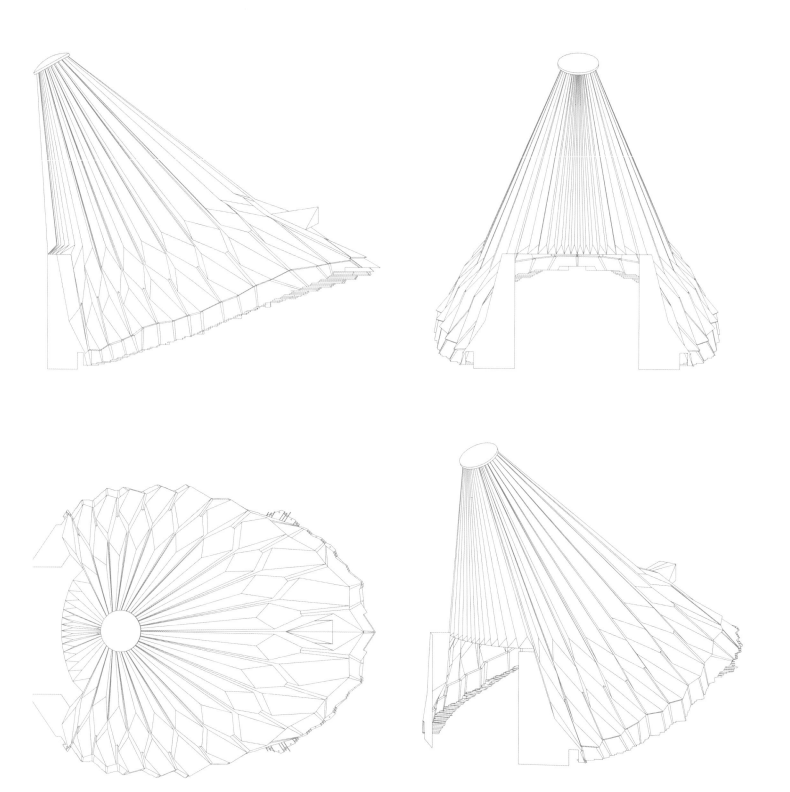

The cone of the concert hall in development (above) and its finished interior (opposite). It is 50 m (164 ft) high. Such an unusual shape is a brave choice for a concert hall, where reliable acoustics are crucial.

Client
Cabildo Insular de Tenerife
Capacity
1660 (concert hall)
428 (chamber hall)
Area
17,300 sq. m/190,000 sq. ft
Cost
Not available

NATIONAL THEATRE OF JAPAN
SHIN TAKAMATSU ARCHITECT & ASSOCIATES
OKINAWA, JAPAN 2003

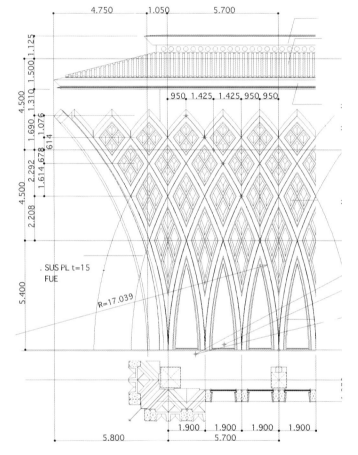

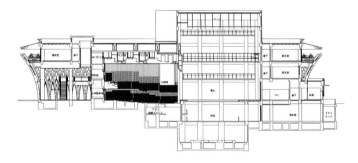

Many aspects of this project's inception suggested that a traditional, even conservative, building would be created for the new National Theatre of Japan. The special committee that had been set up to oversee the project was known to favour traditional architecture, although ostensibly they were unbiased. They decided to construct the building on Okinawa, one of the islands of the Ryukyu chain which, like much of Japan, has a rich cultural life, in particular in the dramatic arts. Much of this is very traditional, such as the *Kumiodori* dance drama, the origins of which date back some three hundred years. The committee chose to build the theatre in the port district of Urasoe in order to hasten regeneration in this rundown area.

The Kyoto-based architect Shin Takamatsu had amassed a vast and diverse portfolio over twenty-five years, although he had not yet built a large-scale performing-arts project. His early buildings have been likened to 'industrial machinery', but the demanding brief for this project asked for a much more sensitive approach. Despite being a new building, the theatre had to reflect both the deep-rooted Japanese culture and the local architecture. Another example of such a combination of old and new is the Tempodrom in Berlin (pp. 48–51), the Modernist form of which successfully fused its heritage of tent arenas with the latest construction methods. Takamatsu addressed these issues in the form and fabric of the building, not simply by superficial or passing reference but in a way that fundamentally affected the design. This has resulted in a unique building, born of its surroundings.

The exterior is dominated by the huge concrete lattice walls running the length of the theatre. Their monumentality is lightened, though, by the space between the walls and the roof, which creates an illusion of the latter as floating, and by the softening of the arched openings in the concrete walls with limestone from local quarries. The local housing style is a clear point of reference, and the colour scheme inside the building is inspired by the outfits of *Kumiodori* performers.

Takamatsu explains that one problem for him was the fact that *Kumiodori* performances are traditionally held outside: "The original traditional entertainment of Okinawa does not need a stage. It has been passed down that it should be performed outdoors. Therefore, it has not developed along with the space in which it is performed, as *Kabuki* or opera have. Historical evidence tells us that the *Okansen Odori*, the dance from which *Kumiodori* originated, was performed on the temporary stage in the courtyard of Shuri Castle back in the time of the Ryukyu dynasty. A temporary stage built indoors is still the best solution for performance in contemporary theatres, although the traditional atmosphere is lost. The architect discussed this problem with local performers, instrument players, directors, technicians and researchers, and these discussions resulted in the construction of mock-up stages to find the best solution. I am convinced now that the answer was to make a stage with a playhouse feel to roam around within the theatre." The interior finishes are of cherry and cypress wood, to imitate as closely as possible the feeling of an outside stage.

Takamatsu drew much inspiration from the surrounding landscape, with its low houses constructed from limestone and red tiles (*kawara*) – materials that withstand heat and typhoons – and Shuri Castle, once home of the Ryukyu kings and now restored to its former glory. As Takamatsu explains, "the traditional houses of Okinawa are an accumulation of historical elements such as *amahaji*, a unique space under the eaves, and *chinibu*, a delicate extension wall made with braided bamboo. This extraordinary work of art is the fruit of thousands of years of enduring the severe island climate, and is also an authentic symbol of Okinawan taste. Full attention to the nature of Okinawan houses simply helped me to satisfy the second criterion of the brief. One could call this a polarization of analogy, an expression of traditional Okinawa using modern materials. I chose to follow the presentiment that modernity gives more impact."

Top left: The exterior detailing is based on a pattern of interlocking pointed arches.

Left: The highly unusual, outwards-leaning walls hide a conventional theatre layout.

Right: The façade resembles a traditional bamboo screen, but on an enormous scale, dwarfing the tiny entrance block.

Left: Like the façades, wall-finishes in the foyer are also influenced by traditional bamboo screens.

Opposite: The auditorium is finished in wood. Modern technology, though present, is un-obtrusive, and the hall is very simply designed.

Client
Okinawa General Bureau of the Government of Japan

Capacity
632 (large theatre)
255 (small theatre)

Area
7,200 sq. m/77,500 sq. ft

Cost
£55m/$92m/€79m

LONDON COLISEUM
ARTS TEAM
LONDON, UK 1904/2004

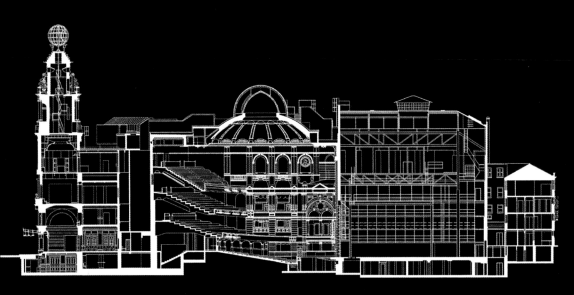

The refurbishment of the Coliseum has included the simplification of the circulation, not an easy task in such an old-fashioned building (above), and the restoration of the glazed roof of the upper circle bar (right).

Originally built by Frank Matcham in 1904, and his greatest achievement, the Grade II*-listed London Coliseum had fallen into disrepair after almost a century of use. The task of restoring the building, now home to the English National Opera (ENO), was a daunting prospect for its owners, particularly in the wake of the long and painful restoration of London's Royal Opera House. That building's extended closure had resulted in significant losses of revenue and possibly damaged the relationship with its faithful audiences. So the ground rules were set for London architects Arts Team (working with Arup Acoustics): minimal downtime and a sympathetic refurbishment.

Matcham's work was not admired during his lifetime (1854–1920), when he was seen as a volume purveyor of 'cheap and cheerful' variety halls. In fact he was quite unpopular during the late Victorian and early Edwardian periods, when he churned out some 150 projects, mostly as part of the era of Oswald Stoll's many 'Empire' theatres. The most notable of these is the Hackney Empire, in east London, which was built three years before the Coliseum and restored at the same time. It is only recently that Matcham has been appreciated, not for his architecture *per se*, but for getting it right. The ornate Coliseum was built in just twelve months – and it worked. He understood theatres and their complex requirements: sightlines, acoustics, ventilation and flow of people. Even when the Coliseum's function changed when the ENO took over in 1968, it still performed. But a century after its construction, many of its attributes – WCs, bars, ventilation, disabled access and acoustics – did not come up to the expectations of increasingly discerning audiences.

To support the application for funding from the Arts Council and Heritage Lottery Fund, a detailed conservation plan was drawn up by theatre historian John Earl. This document set a framework for the restoration and established guidelines for the architect. Refreshingly, Westminster planners and English Heritage, who advise the British government on the historic environment, agreed that any entirely new works should be contemporary and contrasting. The scope of the restoration was broad, from the replacement of sculpted lions 1.5 m (5 ft) high, through glazed roof conservatories, new staircases and a host of specialist mechanical and

electrical services, to a full reinstatement of the original colour scheme.

Most visible of the improvements was the re-creation of a glazed vault over the upper circle bar (Matcham's had been dismantled in the 1960s). High-performance aluminium and energy-efficient glass were used to meet modern regulations and provide a contrast to the ornate original.

Accessibility was a key issue, as two thousand of the ENO's regular visitors have a disability of some kind. Funding agencies are increasingly requiring the provision of comprehensive facilities for the disabled as part of their approval process. David Bonnett, access consultant for the project, explained, "Matcham's preoccupation with separate entry, internal circulation and seating based on ticket price led to an unusually complex circulation system, which has been clarified." This is graphically illustrated in the treatment of the balcony, originally accessed by a winding stone stairway leading up from a side alley. The balcony is now integrated into the main circulation space and has its own bar overlooking the glazed upper circle bar. "It is fitting that [Matcham's] original lift at the ENO, now renewed, was a major component of its new access and evacuation strategy. The elegance of employing such conservation measures as a means of improving accessibility adds credibility to the design team's approach."

The task of restoring the original finishes fell to Clare Ferraby. In the 1960s the brightly coloured, ornate decoration had been painted out in a drab stone colour offset by blue-green carpet and William Morris wallpaper. She explains her approach: "Auditoria are complex, viewed at first with carefully defined house lighting; then, as the lights dim, the form will modify to focus towards the performance, with the deeper recesses disappearing while the faces around tiers in boxes and critical elements of the defining form of the inner space remain, gradually lit by reflected light off the stage."

The architects were successful in minimizing downtime during the works, with a total of just forty-six weeks of lost performance time in a twenty-four-month contract period.

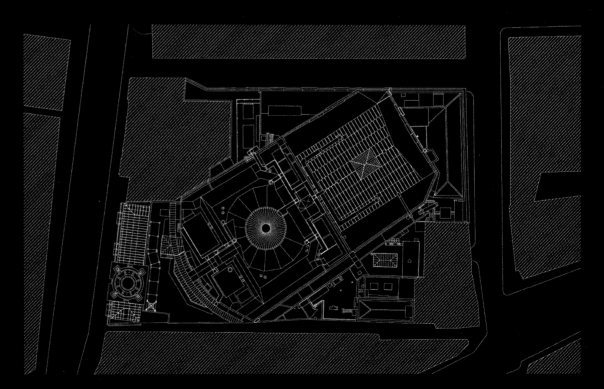

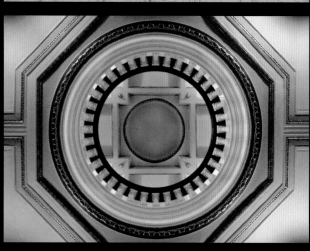

The sumptuous finishes of Frank Matcham's interior have been lovingly restored. The decoration has been returned to its original colour scheme of Imperial purple, Italian reds, and shades of gold and cream.

Client
English National Opera
Capacity
2358
Area
Not available
Cost
£41m/$75m/€62m

JAY PRITZKER PAVILION, MILLENNIUM PARK
GEHRY PARTNERS
CHICAGO, USA 2004

Frank Gehry's first building in Chicago is the centrepiece of the city's new $475m Millennium Park, a brave attempt at creating a vibrant public space in what can only be described as a concrete jungle. The building is a new home for the city's Grant Park Symphony Orchestra, which for nearly seventy years has been providing free summer concerts in downtown Chicago, and it is dedicated to Chicago's Pritzker family, owners of Hyatt Hotels and the Marmon Group, and key proponents of the project.

Known as the 'windy city' because of the icy winds that blow off Lake Michigan, Chicago is a weather-beaten and inscrutable place. This project is an attempt to counteract decades of commercially driven development and produce a focal point, a 'Central Park' experience for the city's residents.

The Millennium Park project is classic brownfield urban regeneration, built partially on the site of the previous public space, over a municipal car park, and partially on the disused nineteenth-century Illinois Central Railroad tracks. Michigan Avenue's powerful wall of skyscrapers to the west dominates the park, which is built one level up from the street; nearly a mile long, this avenue is lined with such classic

nineteenth-century edifices as Daniel Burnham's Railway Exchange Building and the Auditorium Building by Louis Sullivan and Dankmar Adler.

Gehry's first proposal for the site paid homage to the austere principles of structure and form of Ludwig Mies van der Rohe's Chicago architecture. This conservative design disappointed the client, however, who was unashamedly seeking the 'Bilbao effect' – the tremendous critical acclaim, publicity and financial boost provided by Gehry's Guggenheim Museum in Spain and his more recent Walt Disney Concert Hall in Los Angeles (pp. 116–19). In their eyes, this could only be delivered by one of Gehry's trademark 'titanium specials'. The resulting design is clearly derived from the Guggenheim, but lacks the integrity of its forerunner. Only the lower sections of the sculptural, billowing forms are functional, directing sound towards the audience; acoustics are otherwise artificially enhanced by electronic amplification.

Another striking element is the structure of steel tubes, rather like a tent frame, that radiates from the bandstand; but again its function is not immediately apparent. At first glance it could be the support for a retractable canopy to cover the seating,

but, although it spans the seating area, its function is in fact to hold the speakers required to distribute the amplified sound. This overbearing framework detracts to some degree from the dramatic juxtaposition of Gehry's curvy, vivacious architecture with the hard lines of the skyscrapers behind. The rear of the building is an exposed mass of scaffold-like structures supporting the billowing form at the front. This feature has been tenuously justified as homage to Chicago's architectural tradition of form expressing structure, but some have argued that the building is really just a big façade.

And big it certainly is. To host the city's Fourth of July concert and numerous pop festivals, the pavilion provides fixed seating for 4000, and the great lawn extending from it accommodates a further 7000. Whether Gehry had crossed the line from architecture to art with this project was irrelevant to the tens of thousands of visitors who poured into the park on the afternoon of its opening, clearly revelling in the excitement of his dramatic design.

Also designed by Gehry, the BP Bridge, a structure of stainless steel and wood, snakes across Columbus Drive, shielding the pavilion from the noise of the busy road and connecting it to the green spaces on Chicago's lakefront. Finally, Anish Kapoor's *Cloud Gate* sculpture and Jaume Plensa's *Crown Fountain* complete the top-line billing of the park.

Client
City of Chicago
Capacity
4000 (can be extended to 7000)
Area
8800 sq. m/95,000 sq. ft
Cost
£33m/$60.3m/€50m

Pages 86–87: Gehry's flowing design provides a stark contrast to the harsh backdrop of Chicago skyscrapers.

Right: The tubular-steel framework supports the sound systems.

ORIENTAL ART CENTRE
PAUL ANDREU
SHANGHAI, CHINA 2004

Opposite: The Oriental Art Centre's unique shape sets it apart from other buildings in the metropolis.

Right top and centre: The auditoria, each with a gleaming skin of glass and aluminium, loom over the surrounding streetscape.

Bottom: The clover-leaf arrangement of the 'teacups' is apparent in the site plan. All three halls are accessed from a central area.

In the shape of giant teacups, Paul Andreu's Oriental Art Centre grows out of the earth. The focus on the base of the building is one of his fundamental design principles for this project: "The base is the place for preparations for everyone involved in making the shows. The auditoriums are rooted in it. This is a functional necessity, of course, but also a telling expression of the way in which creative work, preparations and rehearsals underpin the moment of encounter."

Andreu's fusion of inspirational design and pragmatic approach probably won the day with the competition panel. However, he may never know as he is not even sure who was on the jury panel or what in particular attracted them to his scheme. He believes that ultimately a jury has to gain confidence in the architect from what they have seen, and to reach the conclusion that the proposal contains enough good elements to prove that he is capable of solving other problems and delivering the required building. Andreu explains, "Some of the best qualities of a building only come out as the project develops, and [the jury has] to anticipate that." The competition had a two-tier entry system: the shortlist consisted of seven entries for which a fee was paid, but any other architect could enter unpaid. Andreu was not one of the seven paid entrants, and he praises the system that clearly gives opportunities to outsiders.

Despite the common misconception that they are bogged down in bureaucracy, the Chinese are in fact able to move very fast by mobilizing their vast labour resource, and the Shanghai project opened in a little over four years. Andreu says this acceleration of construction was a deliberate attempt by the authorities to give an impression of energy to the public.

Moving on from the heady inspirational concepts, Andreu had to deliver a building that worked on all levels. Few buildings present as many challenges for an architect as a performing-arts house, with its two contrasting zones: front of house, all glamour and glitz, managing large numbers of people; and back of house, with the technical demands of air-conditioning, logistics, acoustics and lighting. These support services are vital for a building of this scale with three primary spaces – a 1979-seat concert hall, 1200-seat opera hall and 330-seat chamber-music hall – and a host of ancillary facilities including an exhibition hall, music shops, a restaurant and arts library, and multimedia and training areas.

Managing the circulation efficiently within the organic form is just one of Andreu's accomplishments here. Resisting

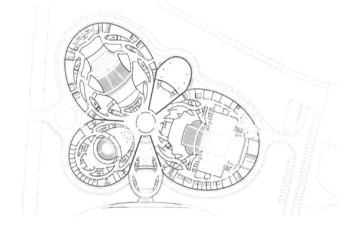

the temptation of regimented grids, his design cleverly disguises a concentric order that is evident only when studying the plans. This was put to the test when, after Andreu had won the competition, the client requested that the 1000-seat theatre originally planned should become a 1200-seat opera hall. The geometry and fluidity of Andreu's design allowed him to do this with "reasonable" ease.

He is fascinated with moments in history when new technology impacts on traditional methods, and when for a period the two are combined in a state of confused flux before the technology is fully accepted and the process changes forever. "It's moments like the end of the nineteenth century had been [in the West]; men with hand tools, and steel and mechanization coming. At that moment we have a very peculiar fragment of history with past and future combined but then – away it goes." He has tried to capture this "moment" inside the centre by combining ceramic, an ancient Chinese medium, with modern materials and fixing technology. The type of ceramics used took a year to develop, in the face of growing opposition from some quarters, but Andreu was passionate about their historical importance and desperately wanted to find a new way of integrating them into the design. He explains, "They are still decorated by hand, and they have many hands. The design incorporates some twenty different repeated elements. People in Europe would laugh at us if we wanted to do the same thing."

The building's three main exterior 'teacup' envelopes are constructed from a special type of glass diffused with perforated aluminium sheet that reduces incidental light transmission at higher levels. This gives the building its 'other-worldly' appearance. Andreu describes his intention: "They house and protect [the performances] as one might protect [something] precious and fragile." Creating this sense of fragility on a building of this magnitude is another indication of Andreu's achievement.

Left: Shanghai's skyline is visible from the internal promenade.

Bottom left: The modern glass and aluminium cladding of the 'teacup'-shaped volumes.

Right: The concert hall, the largest of the three spaces, is clad internally with pear wood.

Client
Shanghai Pudong
New Area
Capacity
1979 (concert hall)
1200 (opera theatre)
330 (chamber hall)
Area
40,000 sq. m/430,500 sq. ft
Cost
£86m/$157.4m/€130m

COPENHAGEN OPERA
HENNING LARSENS TEGNESTUE
COPENHAGEN, DENMARK 2004

Above: The building has become an iconic structure in Copenhagen.

Right: The opera house aligns with the Amalienborg axis: the dome of the Frederikskirken can be seen across the water.

Bottom left and right: The opera house offers spectacular views of the city.

Opposite: The glazed foyer is particularly dramatic.

This is undoubtedly the fastest-built opera house in the world, catapulted from concept to completion by a unique set of circumstances in an unprecedented four years. Snøhetta's National Opera House in Oslo (pp. 188–91) was begun well before, but Copenhagen was completed when Oslo was still at the groundwork stage. While it was refreshing for the architect to bypass the typically long-drawn-out process of creating an opera house, the speed at which this building developed was frightening in its potential for disaster.

In 2000, Henning Larsens Tegnestue (HLT) was commissioned to investigate the possibilities of redeveloping Copenhagen's run-down harbour area, and to set out plans for it. The architects recommended a mixed-use scheme incorporating three major cultural institutions, possibly a theatre, an arena and a museum. The basis of their plan was to turn the focus of the city towards the water, so they included a pier that would allow ferries to connect the parts of the city historically separated by the river.

Soon after it submitted the plan, HLT was approached by Maersk Mc-Kinney Møller, the owner of one of the world's largest fleets, who wanted to fund a public building for the city of Copenhagen. His only condition was that he would be the

sole donor. After a series of exploratory discussions, it was decided that the building would be an opera house. Mr Møller would not offer the building to the city unless he was sure they would agree to it, so after a secret meeting with the prime minister he made a formal proposal, which was duly accepted. He was accustomed to commissioning tankers, however, which take nine months to construct, and did not see why an opera house should be any different. Aged ninety-two at the time, he was also determined that he should see the result. Setting a furious pace, he gave the architects fourteen days to produce sketch designs for the official press launch of the building that would change the face of Denmark's capital.

HLT flew a team around the world to see what was currently happening in the public building arena. One of the projects they visited was Jean Nouvel's Cultural and Conference Centre in Lucerne, Switzerland, which has clearly provided the inspiration for the roof of the Copenhagen building. A suitably prominent location was chosen, and the cantilever, which oversails the main

structure by some 30 m (98 ft), also provided the waterfront focus that HLT believed was fundamental to the project.

Despite the ridiculous timeframe, HLT not only created a stunning design but also wove the new building inextricably into its context, centring it on a projected extension of the Amalienborg axis. This old street has at one end the Frederikskirken on the other side of the river, a building that had itself been donated to the city; and it passes through a large plaza roughly halfway between the church and the new opera house. The alignment is evident from many vantage points around the building as well from the church. It was never anticipated that the opera house would stand alone, but rather that it would be a part of the integrated waterfront development; but there have been delays with the substantial residential blocks to the north and south that HLT had planned to balance the massing of such a large building, and the opera house currently looks rather isolated.

The massive roof extends over the entrance plaza, which affords 180° views

along the harbour from the Knippels Bridge to the south, over the city centre with its towers and spires to the northern harbour entrance and the Sound. The enormous glass frontage on this side allows glimpses through the foyer of the violin-shaped auditorium shell clad in stained, lacquered maplewood. The auditorium adopts a classic configuration with parterres and horseshoe galleries (three for the audience and a technical gallery on top). Classic boxes have given way to open balconies, however, for better sightlines and acoustics.

HLT was pragmatic about the skills required to realize such a project, and international specialists were brought in to assist local firms. Many came from London, including engineers from Buro Happold and Arup Acoustics. The first performance took place on 15 January 2005.

Opposite: The sweeping curves of the auditorium surround a stage that can be configured to suit each individual performance.

Below: The oversailing roof is pierced by the theatre tower.

Client
A.P. Møller and Chastine Mc-Kinney Møller Foundation
Capacity
1641
Area
41,000 sq. m/441,000 sq. ft
Cost
£221.5m/$405.4m/€335m

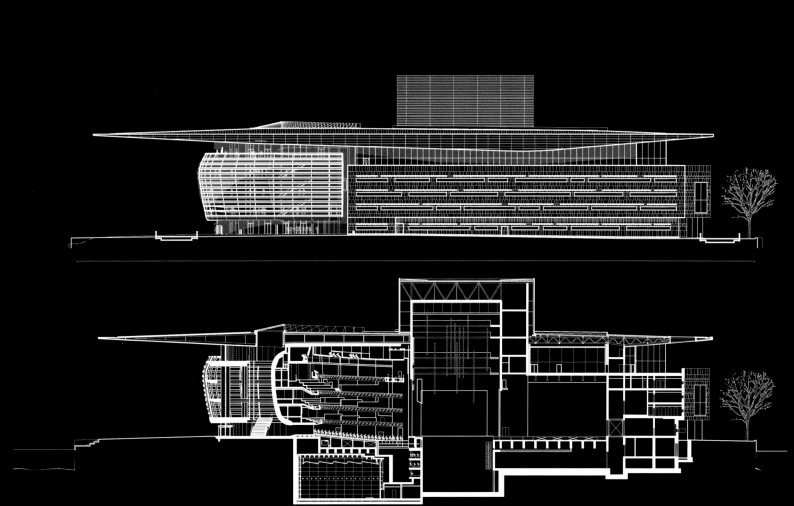

Dwindling congregations and escalating maintenance costs have combined over the past few decades to test the sustainability of many of the UK's churches. The sight of these once magnificent buildings now redundant and boarded up is becoming increasingly common, and is a graphic indication of our changing times. They present an interesting dilemma for planners, as many are listed but at the same time present a unique opportunity for architects. Eastgate Scottish Episcopal Church, built in 1871 in Peebles, in the Scottish Borders, was one such example. Pressure to put the church to new use was increasing in the town, however, with some nineteen arts groups looking for a home. They finally came together in 1995 to create a group called 'Under one roof'. The district council set up a company, Borders1996, which became the fundraiser and client, but it would take several years to complete the project.

Architect Richard Murphy, who had recently completed the Dundee Contemporary Arts Centre and the Stirling Tolbooth, was undaunted by the enormous challenge of Eastgate, and looked at the project with relish. He was going to have to work almost entirely within the constraints of the existing fabric of the Grade II-listed structure, but believed strongly that "the presence of the theatre should be evident from the exterior rather than simply discovered inside an otherwise unchanged church". A key element of the building's success would be its transparency to the street outside, to entice passers-by.

Murphy's solution was suitably dramatic. The east elevation was removed almost entirely and replaced with contemporary glazing, with the roof supported by unashamedly industrial steel. This provided the required link to the street and allowed views into the vibrant café, immediately bringing the building to life. The contemporary east elevation is a bold contrast to the Victorian Gothic façade, clearly fulfilling Murphy's aim to "allow the developing history of the building to be understood so that both eras of its construction sit in creative juxtaposition with each other".

What the project lacks in size (it is a mere 840 sq. m/9000 sq. ft), it makes up for in complexity. One of the many challenges involved was how to accommodate the diverse requirements of the various groups to be housed there. A significant degree of multi-tasking was needed from the building. Space was also a major challenge: as well as being extremely limited, it was the wrong shape and in the wrong places. Evidence of this could be seen all over the building, but Murphy has cunningly adapted his design to use every inch. The main auditorium has benches that can be

EASTGATE THEATRE AND ARTS CENTRE
RICHARD MURPHY ARCHITECTS
PEEBLES, UK 1871/2004

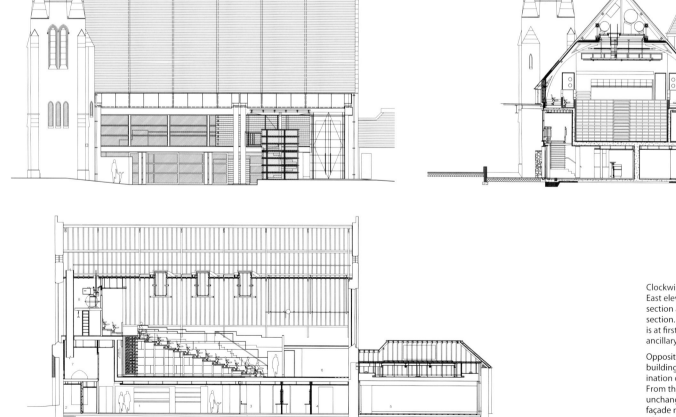

Clockwise from top left: East elevation, cross-section and longitudinal section. The auditorium is at first-floor level, with ancillary spaces beneath.

Opposite: The refurbished building is a bold combination of old and new. From the front it appears unchanged, but the east façade reveals the extent of the conversion.

removed to provide floor space for dances and even jumble sales. The ground-floor café has to double as a foyer, the air-handling plant and lighting services are jammed into the triangular spaces in the apex of the roof, and, most impressively, a lift can also be used as vital stage space. In summer the glazed screen to the foyer slides away so that the café occupies the new lowered section of the side street. A fire escape from the auditorium is expressed as an almost freestanding Parisian poster bollard on the pavement. This feature also divides the façade into front of house and backstage, there being no access elsewhere for scenery delivery.

The theatre has to accommodate a huge range of performances, including chamber music, professional touring theatre, films, local amateur productions and mass events such as the Christmas pantomime. It may well have an extra use: managers are hoping that its proximity to Edinburgh, which has a severe shortage of rehearsal space, will mean that it becomes a venue for performers in the run-up to the hugely successful annual Fringe Festival. By tapping into the vibrancy of such a major cultural city, Eastgate has a unique opportunity to work at two levels, providing both a facility for local groups and the chance to see international-quality performances at a local venue.

Opposite: The original east façade was removed and replaced with a glass wall that can be slid back in fine weather. The round metal structure houses a fire escape and separates access to backstage areas from the café terrace.

Above: The auditorium has been cleverly fitted into the available space. The church's high ceiling accommodates lighting gantries.

Client
Eastgate Theatre & Arts Centre (Borders1996)

Capacity
220

Area
840 sq. m/9000 sq. ft

Cost
£2m/$3.7m/€3m

THE SAGE GATESHEAD
FOSTER AND PARTNERS
GATESHEAD, UK 2004

Along with the wonderful Millau Viaduct in France and the 30 St Mary Axe office tower in London (which won the 2004 Stirling Prize), the Sage Gateshead – his first performing-arts project – cemented Norman Foster's position as the UK's most famous architect, capable of designing any type of building. Standing on the south bank of the River Tyne, the Sage (named after its sponsor, the accounting software company, and designed in partnership with Arup Acoustics) has some high-profile neighbours: Wilkinson Eyre's Millennium Bridge and the Baltic Centre for Contemporary Art by Ellis Williams Architects. Its amorphous, curvaceous shape – inspired by the familiar arches of the original Tyne Bridge, which is known by locals as the 'coat hanger' – contrasts with the industrial rectilinear mass of the Baltic and the slender, sculptural bridge. A single flowing roof unifies the three halls, the shapes of which can be detected beneath it.

The three auditoria all have specific functions. The largest, Hall One, is a classic 1700-seat 'shoebox' hall with a fixed platform that caters primarily for chamber orchestra performances, and can be extended for larger symphony orchestras. Acoustic flexibility is achieved by the use of six gargantuan ceiling slabs weighing some 14 tonnes each, which can be adjusted in height from 10 to 21 m (33 to 70 ft). Motorized sound-absorption panels can be deployed to cover 90 per cent of the wall area. As Foster explains, the concert hall is one of the hardest-working building types, possibly even more so than such others as the hospital and the airport, because everything has to perform: "Every surface material and texture is there for a reason. All the timber surfaces in the room are shaped to provide optimum sound diffusion. The timber is very thick and/or directly bonded to the concrete structure to prevent unwanted low-frequency sound absorption. Wall surfaces incorporate a convex curvature (for low-frequency sound diffusion) and the timber battens diffuse the middle- and high-frequency sounds. All other surfaces, including the balcony fronts and ceilings, also incorporate curvature and shaping to help promote sound diffusion."

The second hall, Hall Two, had an unusual brief. As well as providing a stage for classical chamber music, as part of the repertoire of Northern Sinfonia, it was to be the home of the Sage Gateshead's other principal

Left: The curving roof echoes the form of the Tyne's famous 'coat hanger' bridge.

Opposite: The glazed west elevation houses the entrance to the complex.

group, Folkworks, which is the UK's leading folk music organization, rooted in the Northumbrian pipes, fiddles and accordion music of the region. Jazz, in its many forms, is also performed in this hall. The galleried space holds 400 people on three levels, with a five-sided form at stage-level opening out into a ten-sided one above. The decagonal form satisfies the acoustic requirements and provides an intimate but well-sized space in which artists can experiment with music and musical theatre.

The Northern Rock Foundation Hall is a smaller, 200–300-seat 'shoebox' hall

intended primarily as rehearsal space for the Northern Sinfonia. It has been designed to match the acoustic characteristics of the larger hall, although its natural acoustics are also suitable for small groups of performers.

A large concourse provides a public focus to the building with its cafés, bars, shops, box office, a music information and education centre, and informal performance spaces.

The centre's over-arching roof, designed by Buro Happold, is entirely independent of the auditorium volumes, and is supported by four structural steel arches spanning 80 m (263 ft) from north to south with a secondary structure of single-radii steel members. The 720-tonne steel grid is covered with 3000 linen-finish steel and 280 glass cladding panels. All the cladding panels are flat and the 12,000 sq. m (130,000 sq. ft) surface area is the minimum possible, to keep costs down.

Great attention has been paid to minimizing the building's impact on the environment, and only the auditoria are artificially air-conditioned, although the need for absolute quiet in these spaces meant that the plant had to be housed separately. Cooled air is fed through large ducts to the seating pedestals at 0.5 m (1½ ft) per second, the lowest possible air-flow. The prevailing south-westerly winds provide natural ventilation to the concourse and education centre. The concourse, which is north-facing, requires no artificial cooling and its thermal conditions are regulated by a mixed-mode heating and ventilation system. In addition, the mass of the brick and masonry forms of the auditoria is harnessed as thermal storage.

The foyer and Hall Two. The glazed roof structure is entirely independent of the auditoria.

Left and far left: The circulation is clear and open, and views out are available from every direction.

Below left: Every element of the largest hall has been designed for the best possible acoustics.

Opposite: The public spaces can also be used for performance.

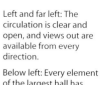

Client
Gateshead Council

Capacity
1700 (Hall One)
400 (Hall Two)
300 (Northern Rock Foundation Hall)

Area
17,500 sq. m/190,000 sq. ft

Cost
£70m/$128m/€106m

THEATRE, SOUTH EAST ESSEX COLLEGE
KSS DESIGN GROUP
SOUTHEND, UK 2004

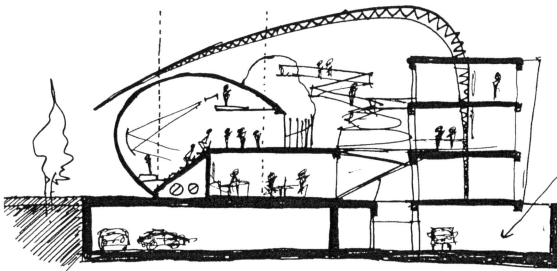

Above: The brief included the design of the college's logo, which is based on the form of the building.

Opposite: The main entrance incorporates open, public space for meeting and socializing.

As part of the regeneration plan for Southend, KSS Design Group were engaged to design a new college on a brownfield site behind the high street, to bring together in one place the functions of five different facilities around the town. The project was to provide a new landmark for the town, and a radical 'high-street store' approach to further education – competing with the sale of holidays and clothes. To achieve this and broaden its audience, certain elements, such as restaurants and the theatre, would also be open to the public during the evenings and at weekends.

South East Essex College is part of a new generation of colleges and academies procured by the UK government under its Private Finance Initiative. It is an interesting result of the increased demand for buildings to be more flexible, in the sense not only of serving different functions, but also of being available to different users. Here, as well as being used as a lecture theatre, the auditorium is used outside college hours for public performances, so that almost all sections of the community can benefit from its facilities at different times.

The scope of the brief for the new college was incredibly wide-ranging, and started from scratch, even requiring a new logo. KSS brought elements of the building into the logo: the red form of the theatre (strikingly shaped like a guitar plectrum) is crossed by the blue line that represents the barrier between the educational and relaxation zones of the college; a line that can even be seen from outside the building.

The architects adopted an organic concept for the new college; although here this so often (ab)used term does not simply refer loosely to any non-rectilinear form. The entire layout is based on the human form, complete with spine, brains and internal organs, and even waste removal. Whether the 'human' concept will work as a fully operating educational machine is yet to be seen, but it is an original approach to the complexities of building layout.

The brief required the provision of a small public performance venue, which would allow people to visit, be entertained and leave without disrupting the life of the college. Describing how this fitted in with the organic theme of the building, Andy Simons, KSS director, explains: "The pod became a lung ... breathing people in and out and providing an interface and exchange without disrupting the remainder of the body. [It even has] a trachea link to the outside." This theatre is acoustically perfect, according to the college's publicity material, and seats 250 people.

Constructed in monocoque form and finished in a brave red, it is housed within a vast lightweight atrium constructed from cushions of EFTE (ethylene tetrafluoro-ethylene, a material much lighter than glass, which was used for the domes of Grimshaw's Eden Project in Cornwall) next to a cluster of *Blade Runner*-style multi-level circular islands that are used for informal lectures, performances and dining. The atrium is split into three areas: the islands and meeting/tutorial spaces; the theatre pod with its integrated moulded seating and sports floor; and the 'forest' zone, an exhibition area and informal meeting space under the dining decks. It has been designed so that it can host large-scale events, with the decks and balconies used as a theatre/cinema and images projected on to the ETFE structure.

A system of natural air circulation heats and cools the spaces using a series of channels in specially constructed concrete planks that are integrated into the structure of the building. The ETFE cushions are more opaque the higher they are, to control solar heat gain as the sun reaches the south-facing atrium each day.

A report by the UK architectural watchdog the Commission for Architecture and the Built Environment (CABE) has found that "the design of buildings can be a key factor in the recruitment of students: that all-important 'wow factor' can increase a college and university's prospect of attracting and retaining both staff and students". Presumably this influence extends to the introduction of 'cool' and accessible performance spaces in the continuing struggle to attract younger theatre- and concert-goers.

Opposite: Futuristic sculptural forms are even used for such functional areas as the dining zone.

Top, above and right: KSS used the idea of 'organic' form literally in the bright red auditorium pod.

Above right: The 'saucers' can be used for performances as well as for dining.

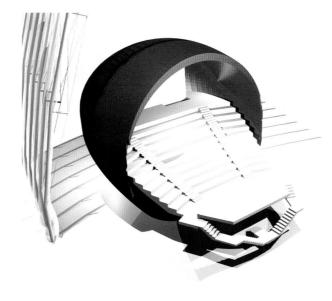

Client
Equion/Laing O'Rourke
Capacity
250
Area
Not available
Cost
£43m/$78.7m/€65m

WALES MILLENNIUM CENTRE
PERCY THOMAS
CARDIFF, UK 2004

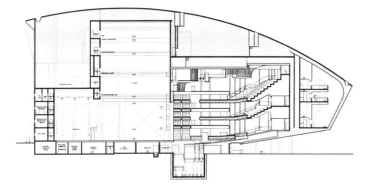

Top and opposite: The cut-out lettering is striking by both day and night.

Above: The cross-section shows the cantilevered volume overhanging the foyer.

As much a symbol of politics as a grand architectural gesture, the Wales Millennium Centre (WMC) was born out of controversy. An earlier scheme by Zaha Hadid for an opera house on the same site was abandoned in 1994 after the organizers lost confidence in Hadid, who came from London and whose work was largely unbuilt at that time. They were also concerned about the identity of the project being affected by the general public's perception of opera as élitist. It was decided instead to build a centre to accommodate musicals, opera and dance, with space for various arts organizations, as well as cafés and gift shops.

Cardiff's harbour area declined after the docks were decommissioned, and the enormous difference between high and low tides (the second greatest tidal range in the world) inhibited development. A barrage built in 1999 eliminated the effect of the tide, creating a freshwater lake and nearly 13 km (8 miles) of waterfront. Despite subsequent regeneration efforts, however, architecture around the bay was incoherent. The mass of the Millennium Centre is far greater than that of any other building here, and it is even bigger than its new neighbour, Richard Rogers' 2005 National Assembly.

Wales is increasingly autonomous within the United Kingdom, and is fiercely proud of its heritage. The brief for the WMC required that the building should express 'Welshness' and that it should be as recognizable as Jørn Utzon's Sydney Opera House. Aside from these demands, Jonathan Adams, project architect for Welsh architectural firm Percy Thomas (now Capita Percy Thomas), was faced with the challenge of producing a building to replace a scheme that had had widespread support from the architectural community.

The profile and form of the centre are certainly distinctive, but unlike the 'Gherkin' label attached to Norman Foster's 30 St Mary Axe, London, public consensus has not yet been reached on a nickname. Adams has used slate to link the building to its Welsh heritage, although he struggled to retain even this dominant feature: successive contractors fought against its use, maintaining that it was impractical. Finally, in a spectacular stand-off, the client was forced to choose between the slate walls and the contractor. The finished building reveals who won.

The building's most distinctive feature is the giant lettering cut out of the curving steel façade to form windows above the main entrance. The message, by Welsh poet Gwyneth Lewis, is predictably conveyed in two languages: "Creu gwir fel gwydr o ffwrnais awen" translates as "Creating truth like glass from the furnace of inspiration";

the lettering in English reads: "In these stones horizons sing." Dominating the façade, this successfully brings a glitzy hint of Broadway into the solid mass of Welsh stone and metal.

Though traditional in appearance, the massive horseshoe auditorium is impressive in scale, second only in size in the UK to London's Royal Opera House. According to Adams, the design of the auditorium reconciles the acoustic requirements outlined by the specialist consultants, Arup Acoustics, with the need for a clear visual organization. "The auditorium can be thought of as a fixed box within which are positioned the sculptural structures of the seating tiers, the side-towers and the ceiling acoustic reflector." These detached structures are all constructed in hardwood and their forms echo the linear patterns of the concourse balconies. The outer walls are lined with fibrous-gypsum tiles and comply with precise sound reflection specifications, with a variety of angled faces that can be combined to give a complex surface.

Reconciling the auditorium's performance and appearance meant repeated acoustic laboratory testing before the materials and shapes could be finalized. The custom-made tiles, coloured a natural earth-red to match the building's other materials, unify the auditorium's outer wall, extending across the faces of the side-slip balconies that alternate with hardwood suspended balconies.

Adams sees the seating as the decisive design element of the auditorium. "The seats for the WMC represent a deliberate move away from theatre convention. Each chair is expressed almost as a separate piece of furniture." The texture of the specially woven materials echoes the architectural geometry, with yarns of different colours to provide natural variation. The colour of the seats changes along important horizontal lines through the auditorium, and this pattern is matched on the retractable acoustic absorption panels with the overall result that the textiles, covering such a large area, are completely integrated with the room's overall architectural treatment.

It is hard to view the centre without wondering what could have been had Zaha Hadid's scheme been realized. Such comparison must be avoided, however, in order to do it justice. Indeed, it would seem that the tide of opinion has turned, with the building receiving accolades. Adams has certainly won the hearts and minds of the Welsh people, who voted the WMC their second favourite building before it had even opened.

Top left: The bar area behind the façade is illuminated during the day through the cut-out letters.

Left: Wood is used extensively throughout the complex.

Opposite: The enormous auditorium with its many balconies offers the audience extremely good sightlines.

Client
Wales Millennium Centre
Capacity
1900 (lyric theatre)
250 (studio theatre)
Area
33,000 sq. m/350,000 sq. ft
Cost
£106m/$194m/€ 160.3m

WALT DISNEY CONCERT HALL
GEHRY PARTNERS
LOS ANGELES, USA 2004

Frank Gehry's Guggenheim Museum in Bilbao, Spain was a pivotal point in his career: its astounding success projected him into the limelight and laid down a course for his subsequent work over which he had very little control. This was graphically illustrated when he tried to create a sympathetic design for a pavilion in Chicago's Millennium Park (pp. 86–89), a design that was immediately rejected by the client as not being enough like that of Bilbao.

The city of Los Angeles had watched one of its citizens magically turn a declining shipyard town in a far corner of Spain into the site of a global cultural icon, and so it was inevitable that Gehry would be prevailed upon to create one of his signature buildings at home. It was also fitting, given the astonishing nature of the 'Bilbao' effect, that this wonderful new landmark should be linked with the world's greatest creator of fairy tales and fantasies.

The stakes were extremely high for Gehry, however: the new building would also have to meet extraordinary technical demands. The Disney family insisted that the hall have an acoustic quality equal to or surpassing those of the best concert halls in the world. Members of the Walt Disney Concert Hall committee and the Los Angeles Philharmonic Orchestra visited auditoria throughout the world and selected halls in Berlin, Amsterdam and Boston as their acoustic ideals. The Philharmonic had also performed several times in Suntory Hall, Tokyo, and liked both the acoustics and the intimacy created by the arrangement of the audience on all sides of the concert platform.

Gehry was already close friends with Ernest Fleischmann, the executive director of the Music Center of Los Angeles County, of whose wider complex the new concert hall would be a part. He spent many evenings with the musicians themselves, meeting composers, conductors and soloists over a long period of time. He then engaged Yasuhisa Toyota of Nagata Acoustics in Tokyo (designer of the Suntory Hall) to work with him on the concept for the hall. A process evolved whereby Gehry produced small-scale models, around thirty in the end, and Toyota evaluated the acoustic

characteristics of each one. Gehry's idea that listening to music is an experience, not just the hearing of sound, led him to consider such different factors as the feel of the seat, and the visual appearance and the temperature of the auditorium all essential to the enjoyment of a great performance.

In the design of this building, as in the case of his Guggenheim Museum, Gehry saw connections with water and, in particular, with sailing. He has likened the design to a "ceremonial barge on which the orchestra and audience take a journey through music". This influence is evident in the sail-like curves of the auditorium ceiling and the flowing forms of the internal walls. Both these features help the sound to disperse, and produce more reflections, adding warmth and resonance.

Gehry has embraced the engineering aspect of his work to a surprisingly large degree, more than most other architects, who rely heavily on engineers to realize their designs. During the design of his fish sculpture for the Barcelona Olympic village in 1992, his partner Jim Glymph came across the specialist 3D software Computer Aided Three-dimensional Interactive Application (CATIA), used to design the French Mirage fighter jet, and Gehry Partners have employed this system ever since. During the construction of the Disney Concert Hall the system was used to send the exact dimensions of each section of cladding directly to the metal cutters, as no two pieces were identical. Once manufactured, the panels were coded and the builders used the same software to install them. The application of gleaming stainless steel cladding was not entirely straightforward, though. Local residents complained about the glare, and following an analysis of the building's surface the offending areas were sanded.

The new 1.8 ha (4.5 acre) site brings the total area of the Music Center complex to 4.5 ha (11 acres). Encompassing a full block in the downtown district of the city, it also contains two outdoor amphitheatres (with 300 and 120 seats), a space for pre-theatre performances, a 250-seat multi-use theatre, and a 280 sq. m (3000 sq. ft) art gallery.

The sweeping panels so characteristic of recent Gehry buildings are all engineered by the architect.

The Walt Disney Concert Hall is a much more welcoming structure than the austere buildings among which it sits; there is little distinction between its precincts and the public area surrounding the venue.

Client
Los Angeles Philharmonic
Capacity
2275
Area
18,500 sq. m/200,000 sq. ft
Cost
£150m/$274m/€ 226.4m

PALACE OF THE ARTS
SANTIAGO CALATRAVA
VALENCIA, SPAIN 2004

Around the time that Santiago Calatrava was born (in 1951), his home city of Valencia was suffering catastrophic flooding. The results of these unconnected events were to come together some fifty years later to change the face of Spain's third largest city. In response to the floods, the regional authority embarked on an incredibly adventurous urban experiment: they would take away the source of the problem, the River Turia, which ran through the heart of the city. Plans were drawn up to divert it around the city and convert the old riverbed into Valencia's own 'Central Park'. Once the lifeblood of the city and arguably the reason for its existence, the river is now a barely noticeable canal-like backwater flowing around Valencia's industrial outskirts. The experiment has clearly been an engineering success, as the flooding has stopped. However, Jardin Turia, as the park made from the old riverbed was officially named (it is known by the locals as the 'green lung'), has sanitized the city centre. Something is missing. Insufficient imagination and resources were applied to realizing the 'Central Park' vision, and the result is a rather motley collection of municipal fountains and playgrounds.

During the closing years of the last millennium, the city realized that it had two unexploited assets: one of its citizens had evolved into a world-class architect, creating magnificent, sculptural architecture in far-flung places; and it had a vast tract of under-used land flowing through its centre. As Barcelona had been transformed into a cultural attraction by Antoní Gaudí (1852–1926), so Valencia would be rejuvenated by Calatrava. In the second major urban experiment, the dry riverbed became Calatrava's playground. It started with a bridge (as the corridor is still treated as a river), then an arts complex and museum, cinema and sea-life centre. This string of buildings, known as the 'City of Arts and Sciences', is located on the wider part of the riverbed as it nears the Mediterranean. A cluster of tall apartment buildings is also planned nearby. The 'city' is impressive, its structures huge and wonderfully Calatrava-esque, but it must be said that it is somewhat lacking in cohesion. There is no apparent narrative of geometry or form and they appear simply to have been randomly set down.

The vast and dominating hulk of the opera house resembles a helmet to some, a giant cockroach to others, with hints of its smaller sister in Tenerife (pp. 72–77) but lacking that building's clear, bird-like simplicity. Its exterior is formed of two vast shells wrapping round the building and coming to a point at each end. Over the top is a tapered roof typical of Calatrava's designs, which in another location could be a bridge. The centre section of the shell cladding on each side has been cut away to expose the structure's inner workings, with vast curves of concrete sweeping around the main auditorium. These form the upper public spaces and provide panoramic views of Valencia and the Jardin Turia snaking through the city.

The scale and form are impressive, of course, but this is chiefly a building of surprises. From every aspect, the building changes: from an ocean liner to an echo of Frank Lloyd Wright's Guggenheim Museum in New York, to something entirely different again. The engineer in Calatrava occasionally comes out to play and teases the onlooker. Looking at the join between the 'tectonic plates' on either side, for example, one assumes a confluence of great forces and loads, and expects to see a massive structural connection. Closer examination reveals that it is not even a joint. The plates are set some 10 cm (4 in.) apart, floating in mid-air, and the viewer is left worried that the builders have omitted some vital piece.

Even underground, the structure is impressive, with rows of sculptural columns in the vast catacombs. Above are eleven further levels housing four main auditoria, public areas, restaurants, cafés, foyers, and galleries (with portholes), all of which add to the effect of a giant liner floating down the Turia. Calatrava has certainly produced an extraordinary building, but one that is entirely fitting for its extraordinary location.

Left: The complex resembles an ocean liner, and 'portholes' add to the effect. They hint at the spaces below ground.

Opposite: Cleverly placed glazing creates a different impression again when night falls.

Client
Government of Valencia
Capacity
1,782; 1,617; 388; 386
Area
350,000 sq. m/
3,800,000 sq. ft
Cost
Not available

CASA DA MUSICA
REM KOOLHAAS/OMA
PORTO, PORTUGAL 2005

As would be expected from Rem Koolhaas's first major performing-arts project, the Casa da Musica is full of surprises. This building is a paradox, pushing the boundaries of accepted practice in some areas but embracing it in others. It was originally conceived as a private house, but Koolhaas scaled up the design by 500 per cent and submitted the result to the competition for a grand concert hall in Portugal's second city. The completed 'house of music', with all its twists and quirks, is an exciting example of his current work.

Koolhaas's creation is set within its own space on a square connected to the Rotunda da Boavista, a historic public park close to the centre of the city, and deliberately stands apart from the surrounding cityscape. None of Santiago Calatrava's graceful curves is apparent in this compact building, but its boxy 'airport terminal' appearance belies the creativity woven into its fabric.

Koolhaas was guided by Cecil Balmond, Arup's deputy chairman, in developing the structure (their working relationship dates back some eighteen years). Balmond has earned a reputation for creative engineering, and has helped to realize many structures that seemed impossible to build. Here he introduced two massive parallel walls each 1 m (3 ft) thick, running the length and height of the building, as the primary structure. The main auditorium is suspended between these walls, an arrangement which automatically sound-proofs it; and the smaller auditorium is wedged between one of the walls and the exterior envelope, which takes the form of a layer 400 mm (15¾ in.) thick wrapping around the internal workings.

The use of this structure has allowed a variety of ancillary rooms to be fitted into the void between the main walls and the outer envelope, making for some interesting spaces. Creating a sense of anticipation as visitors pass through the building towards the auditorium itself is an approach used particularly successfully by Renzo Piano in his Niccolò Paganini Auditorium in Parma (pp. 38–41). Koolhaas has also achieved this within the confines of the Casa da Musica, using every trick to compensate for the lack of space. Visitors

Left and above: Koolhaas has used glazing in the auditorium volume (left). At night, the lit windows accentuate the building's distinctive form.

Inset: The floor plan combines the regular form of the main auditorium with the irregular spaces arranged around it.

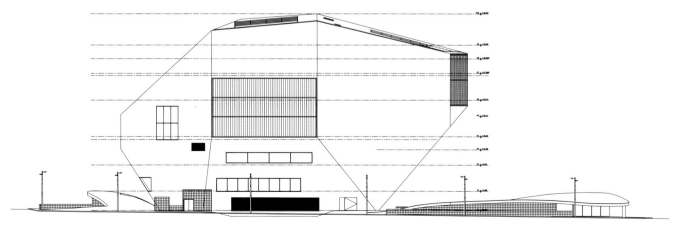

Top left and right: The closed, boxy building is entered through a slot in one side.

Above left: Large windows in unusual places allow light into the heart of the concert hall.

Above right: The building is surrounded by a public plaza and entered by an impressive flight of steps, dramatically lit by night.

Left: The enormous window in the north-west elevation allows views out from high in the building.

climbing the impressive entrance steps from the outside through a slot into the building are surprised when faced with an even grander staircase leading through the void right up into the roof, between the glazed back wall of the auditorium and the window looking out over the city. Contrary to the current trend for vast circulation spaces, though, the ratio of seats to ancillary space here is more reminiscent of that in a Victorian theatre. Koolhaas believes that crush and bustle before a performance will further increase the audience's expectation, enjoyment and sense of event.

Koolhaas has opted for the safe, time-proven 'shoebox' configuration in the main auditorium, but even in such a 'sacrosanct' area there are surprises in store. He has introduced glazing to the end walls, a feature virtually unheard of in performance venues. Acoustician Renz van Luxemburg worked closely with the architect to overcome the many challenges created by the glazing. The glass itself is corrugated, to diffuse reflection, and Petra Blaisse of design company Inside Outside has developed a three-layer curtain system. A knotted curtain filters the light to reduce glare, a dense white curtain with a black lining creates black-out conditions, and an aluminium-coated curtain can be used to increase sound reflection.

The auditorium has to withstand heavy use and accommodate a variety of events – it hosted both rock and orchestral performances on the opening night. This flexibility is partly achieved by the use of an inflatable canopy over the orchestra that reflects sound downwards using a combination of pressure and weight, and which can be adjusted to vary the sound qualities of the hall.

A grey colour scheme pervades the interior, which has provoked comparisons to a backdrop from a Prada catalogue. The seats, which were specially designed by the late Maarten van Severen, blend with this theme; but in the main hall Koolhaas has used gold leaf for a design based on enlarged plywood grain, presumably as a reference to the formwork that created his building. A rooftop restaurant, its floor laid in classic black and white chequers, is open to the Mediterranean sky.

Casa da Musica has made an impact on Porto's skyline and should become one of its major attractions. Koolhaas has shown that he can deliver complex performance spaces and in doing so has placed his work firmly on the world map.

Above: Inside the irregularly shaped building is a 'shoebox' auditorium, conventional in shape if not in decoration.

Left: OMA's finishes create futuristic interiors.

Client
Porto 2001/City of Porto
Capacity
1200 (main auditorium)
350 (smaller auditorium)
Area
30,000 sq. m/
320,000 sq. ft
Cost
Not available

LUXEMBOURG PHILHARMONIC HALL
CHRISTIAN DE PORTZAMPARC
LUXEMBOURG 2005

In 1994, Parisian architect Christian de Portzamparc became France's first winner of the prestigious Pritzker Prize for architecture, and also, at fifty, the youngest ever to be given that award. He went on to design the 1999 LVMH tower in New York, although he is still best known for his City of Music (Cité de la Musique) in Paris, which was completed in 1995.

This latest project, the new home of the Luxembourg Philharmonic Orchestra, comprises a main hall and a number of smaller auditoria. The complex is enclosed within a façade of reed-like appearance, its bold curves belying the rectangular auditorium within. The vertical lines and the boat-like shape are impressive, particularly at night, when the interior light bleeds out, emphasizing the unusual façade treatment.

Portzamparc explains the rationale behind the façade: "When I first looked at the photos of the area, before I had been to see the site, I felt that the public should be led to the future building ... through an initiation zone, a circle of tall trees that one would have to cross to enter the realm of music. When I arrived at the site, I saw that we didn't have enough space to plant trees and this gave me the idea of a filter façade made up of this wooded ring, neither opaque nor transparent, forming a cloak of light with the hall at its centre. The rhythm of these parallel trunks in a number of elliptical ranks became mathematical and musical."

Portzamparc has created an exceptional setting for music ranging from symphonic concerts, solo recitals and jazz to more experimental events with spatially arranged sounds. Each of the three complementary concert halls is designed to provide the best acoustic environment for its function. As with other projects discussed here, such as Michael Wilford's Esplanade National Performing Arts Centre in Singapore (pp. 65–67), the voids between the curved exterior and the rectangular interior form exciting spaces, including,

of course, the main lobby, some 44,450 cu. m (1,570,000 cu. ft) in volume.

It is with the 1500-seat auditorium that Portzamparc makes a bold departure. By adding eight lateral tower galleries to the sides of a traditional shoebox concert hall, he imitates the qualities of an Elizabethan theatre while keeping the benefits of the shoebox's proven acoustics. "I wanted the walls of this hall to be inhabited so as to surround the musicians, to find the relationship with the audience that is found in Shakespeare's theatre. I also wanted imagination to roam so that one would not feel closed in; grandeur must be associated with intimacy. This is why the side walls of the hall are little towers of tiers of boxes, like buildings in the night around a public square."

The smaller, chamber-music hall is enclosed by elegantly curved walls; and these, together with a sound reflector above the stage, create a unique and intimate room for 300 listeners. "The chamber music hall is set in a leaf that unfurls from the ground and rises against the colonnade; it plays with the filter, masking it diagonally, and this game of contrast between opaque and transparent endorses the unity of the project. I love creating architecture for music ... I feel that it expresses the dialogue between two realms of perception, hearing and sight, which respond to one another freely. There is a grace of space. The emotion of music is the discovery of and gradual entry into a different world, a world that reveals itself in time. I understand space too as a phenomenon that we perceive in our movement, with its expectation, its surprises, its connections."

The third and smallest hall is a flexible space for up to 120 people. It is perfect for a wide variety of musical experiences, from experiments in the fields of electronics, film, video and art to interactive workshops for children and young people.

The chamber-music hall is a dramatic and unusual space for smaller concerts. Hanging above the stage is a sculptural but entirely functional sound reflector.

The distinctive façade
is characteristic of
Portzamparc and gives
the impression that the
auditorium is surrounded
by trees.

Left: The vocabulary of
tree-trunks continues
throughout the interior
detailing.

Opposite: The lateral
tower galleries in
the main auditorium
are inspired by the
architecture of
Elizabethan theatres.

Client
Grand Duchy of
Luxembourg

Capacity
1500 (auditorium)
300 (chamber-music hall)
120 (flexible space)

Area
20,000 sq. m/215,000 sq. ft

Cost
£80m/$146m/€ 120m

SÃO PAULO OPERA HOUSE
OSCAR NIEMEYER
SÃO PAULO, BRAZIL 2005

If Henning Larsens Tegnestue's Copenhagen Opera (pp. 94–97) is the world's fastest-built cultural building, then Oscar Niemeyer's recently completed concert hall in Brazil must rate as the slowest, having taken some fifty years to complete. Of course, it was lack of funds and not slow construction that delayed the delivery of this project, but it is still extraordinary that a plan should be realized so long after its conception.

That the building was designed by Niemeyer, an architect inextricably linked with the Modern Movement and Brazil's cultural heritage, played no small part in the decision to finish it. Ibirapuera Park was inaugurated in 1954 to celebrate the city's 400th birthday. Designed by the forty-seven-year-old Niemeyer together with landscape designer Roberto Burle Marx (1909–1994), it covers an area of nearly 200 ha (500 acres) and is the city's main park. The concert hall was always planned as a major feature and complements other Niemeyer structures in the park, among them museums and the flying-saucer-shaped observatory.

However, controversy is never far away from projects of this nature, and, as in many polluted cities of the twenty-first century, green space in central São Paulo is in very short supply. When plans for the project were published, many residents were incensed to see that trees were to be felled and another precious area of inner-city park sacrificed to the gods of bulldozers and concrete. A huge battle between conservationists and cultural advocates ensued, and the result is indicative of the power that music still holds in this developing Latin city. Even Niemeyer had concerns about the ecological impact of elements of the project, and he wanted to replace an ugly walkway linking the building to the observatory with a garden; but the city council stood firm and so Niemeyer refused to attend the inauguration of the concert hall.

From the outside, the building can only be described as a white wedge. However, Niemeyer has playfully incorporated a huge bright-red 'tongue' that emanates from the entrance, giving a hint of what is to be found inside. Niemeyer has employed this combination of striking red with white concrete before, in his 'bleeding hand' memorial, also in São Paulo, and in the twisting ramped entrance to his 1996 Museum of Contemporary Art at Niterói, Rio de Janeiro, which has a red floor and white concrete walls.

The back wall has a 20-m (66-ft) opening to the stage, giving audiences inside a backdrop of the park and allowing those outside to watch concerts from the grass. Every Sunday morning free concerts will be held for people in the park. This initiative brings the concert hall into line with those of other new buildings where a concern for transparency and inclusion is evident, belying the building's genesis in the 1950s when such issues were not generally considered.

The interior forms a total contrast to the straight lines of the exterior, with curves being the dominant feature of the public spaces. The forms are enhanced by a superficial extension of the decorative red tongue, designed by Tomie Ohtake (mother of Brazilian architect Ruy Ohtake), which weaves around the interior. The result is striking, but some will argue that the overpowering art taints the otherwise pure Modernist sculptural effect.

The auditorium has a capacity of 840. Its rectangular seating configuration makes it rather more formal and conservative than the foyer areas. Red seating, however, provides continuity with the palette used elsewhere. The basement contains a VIP room, a government-funded music school, a café and the dressing rooms.

At the time the concert hall was completed, Niemeyer, aged ninety-seven, was still working in Rio de Janeiro within sight of Copacabana Beach. A man of habit, he is reported to arrive at his small, book-filled office at ten o'clock each morning and start work. On hearing that his concert hall would finally be built, he is said to have scribbled across a sketch of it: "After so many years, the auditorium will be built and the entrance to Ibirapuera finally finished as it should have been."

Above: The interior is dominated by Tomie Ohtake's red sculptural 'tongue'.

Opposite top: The 'back door' allows concerts to be seen and heard by people outside.

Opposite centre: The colour red, which dominates the design, is first encountered as a marker for the entrance.

Opposite bottom: The auditorium is formal and plainly finished.

Client
City of São Paulo

Capacity
840

Area
Not available

Cost
Not available

THE EGG
HAWORTH TOMPKINS
BATH, UK 2005

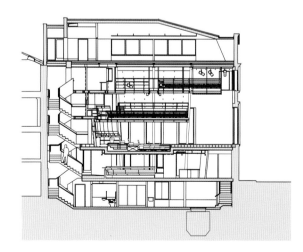

The Victorians may not have considered what uses lay in store for their buildings, but the high quality of their construction means that they are more versatile and hence sustainable than many contemporary structures. Built as a house and then converted to a cinema, this building in historic Bath has once again been gutted, this time for a third life.

The Egg is the third venue for the Theatre Royal, Bath (TRB), and will provide a year-round programme of theatre and performance for and by children and young people. A dedicated space unique in its focus on the 0–25 years age group, it aims to attract up to 45,000 young people each year.

Interestingly for London-based architects Haworth Tompkins, the brief was drawn up with the help of a group of twenty children between the ages of nine and seventeen, to ensure that the Egg meets the needs of the people it is intended to serve. These young people were first taught how to consult, and then sent out to talk to their peers to discover exactly what a children's theatre should be like. A key element of the young client team's brief was the theatre's outward appearance and visibility. The young consultants formulated sophisticated ideas on the importance of physically communicating the theatre's activity to the outside world, and incorporating a café in the design.

Working within the external walls of the existing building (the original interior of which had been all but destroyed by previous conversions) the scheme employs an innovative structural solution to insert a tightly fitting elliptical 120-seat auditorium into the rectangular shell of crumbling Bath stone. The raking steel structure avoids the existing historic building's foundations and respects its original fabric, while informing the auditorium's distinctive and intimate shape. Clad in padded upholstery felt and corrugated red plastic sheeting, the

Opposite top: Concept sketch shows the arrangement of the 'egg' shape inside the building envelope.

Opposite bottom: A cross-section reveals how the programme has been fitted into a fairly restricted structure.

Left: The small auditorium seen from above. The seating is scaled for children.

auditorium has a structural presence that is felt throughout the theatre, as its form protrudes through the ceiling of the ground-floor café.

Mirroring the presence of the TRB's main theatre but reinterpreting it for its young users, the architects have steered clear of the black-box studio approach to theatre design while achieving a high degree of flexibility. Circulation spaces wind around the central intervention from a street-level café up to the rooftop rehearsal room with panoramic views across Bath. Retaining the large existing windows but also fitted with black-out shutters, the auditorium is unique in the UK in enabling both fully day-lit and blacked-out performances, and is usable in end-on, in-the-round, flat-floor and traverse configurations.

The original Bath stone skin of the building forms an important base ingredient in the scheme, against which a palette of brightly coloured and textured contemporary materials play. Marks of demolition and other earlier features on the interior masonry have been retained – though complemented by new structural concrete repairs and openings wherever necessary – to contrast with new materials such as resin flooring, corrugated plastic sheet, mirrored steel and felt.

The all-important café is a specifically child- and family-friendly space. The young people in the consultant team insisted on including it as a social space to encourage a sense of ownership and belonging. The translucent red corrugated plastic sheeting surrounding the auditorium not only creates a sense of intimacy but also has an important lightbox effect. The architects have responded to the request for exterior visibility by projecting coloured light through the façade to the exterior of the building, creating the sense of a glowing ember of activity inside.

Opposite top: The auditorium can be fully day-lit through the large eighteenth-century windows.

Opposite bottom: The curved auditorium has been inserted into the original stone shell.

Clockwise from top left: The child-friendly café features a mirrored ceiling; the fenestration glows red, hinting both at the unusual treatment of the interior and at the activity taking place there; the new theatre has proved popular with children.

Client
Theatre Royal, Bath

Capacity
120

Area
Not available

Cost
£2.3m/$4.2m/€ 3.5m

UNICORN THEATRE FOR CHILDREN
KEITH WILLIAMS ARCHITECTS
LONDON, UK 2005

The purpose of this theatre in the backstreets of London's borough of Southwark strikes at the very heart of the primary issue facing the performing-arts industry today – attracting younger audiences. This pioneering project, the first new theatre dedicated to children in the UK, naturally brought many challenges for the company and the designers. However, the strategy adopted by the architect Keith Williams is refreshing and original.

The Unicorn Theatre for Children was founded in 1947 by Caryl Jenner (1917–1973). The company began by putting on performances from ex-Ministry of Defence trucks for children in isolated communities in Buckinghamshire and Hertfordshire, and subsequently toured the UK. This nomadic existence continued until the 1960s; the company then shared space in the Arts Centre in London's Leicester Square until 1999. During that time the Unicorn established a reputation for producing high-quality performances for children between the ages of four and twelve.

Clearly Williams' sensitivity to the issue of "winning the hearts and minds" of the children played a key part in the selection of his practice. "Children measure their ages in quarter years so it would have been almost impossible to cater for such a wide band, so we devised a grown-up building for them. … Treating the children like adults encourages them to behave more thoughtfully." Williams also had to deal with a client without experience of commissioning architecture: "We … had to provide a building which was the first that the Unicorn had ever had. A building that would enable them to develop as a producing house, rather than a receiving house."

The project had other challenges. In a part of London already undergoing major regeneration and falling within a masterplan created by Foster and Partners, Williams had to use his sensitivity once more, to create an exterior that would maintain a narrative with the adjacent buildings. The site is on the north side of Tooley Street, which runs parallel to the

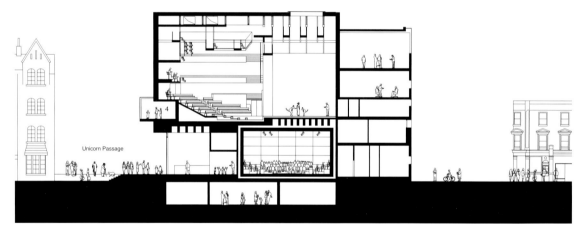

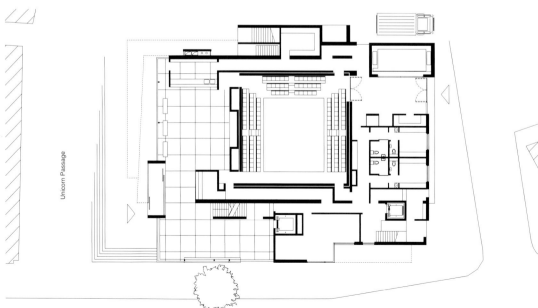

Top and opposite: The façade is broken down imaginatively with a varied palette of materials.

Above right: The auditorium is set above the foyer area.

Right: The ground-floor plan shows the studio space at the centre, with the foyer to the left. The building is entered from Unicorn Passage to the west.

River Thames and some 300 m (980 ft) to the south. This section of riverbank is home to a swathe of new architecture, including Foster's City Hall and other major office buildings seven to ten floors high. The buildings on Tooley Street are at a smaller scale, and the Unicorn, bounding a pedestrianized spine connecting Tooley Street to the river, forms a link between the two relative sizes of building.

The primary requirements of the brief were a new 350-seat theatre, a 120-seat studio space, a rehearsal room, foyers and cafés. Williams had some freedom to use his imagination as the theatre was the only arts building in the block, but the constrained footprint meant that the development would be extremely dense. "We had to cram all this into the building while addressing the urban opportunities, and as with any arts brief there is always a process of meshing the design with expectations and budgets to achieve a solution which is acceptable." An outreach programme established with a local school included workshops with children, many of whom had never been to a theatre. "They asked some difficult questions, and this gave us an opportunity not to lose sight of what the project was all about."

Williams (working with Arup Acoustics) felt strongly that the building should be as transparent as possible at ground level to tempt in passers-by. "That principle was not possible as long as the theatre was on ground level; this gave us the opportunity to explore other ideas based on jacking the auditorium up to first-floor level." The stage was duly set at 8 m (26 ft) above the ground. The studio space snuggles under the theatre and is acoustically separate. The form of the main auditorium, in a copper-covered box 'floating' above the foyer, is clearly inspired in part by that of the classic amphitheatre, and is reached by a theatrical journey up stairs through various levels. A large window allows views into the studio, where workshops are held.

The lack of precedents for designing an auditorium for children that also needed to accommodate accompanying adults resulted in many 'back to first principles' debates. "A seat that is going to be comfortable for a four-year-old is not going to be much use for an adult. We initially explored the idea of batches of 'age-defined' seats but quickly realized that this was not practical as you can't forecast the

Left: The entrance elevation from Unicorn Passage. By being set back from the glass membrane, the structure can be clearly read.

Below left: The cutaway sketch shows the importance given to the theatre's public areas.

Right: The main auditorium is fitted with bench seating to accommodate both children and adults.

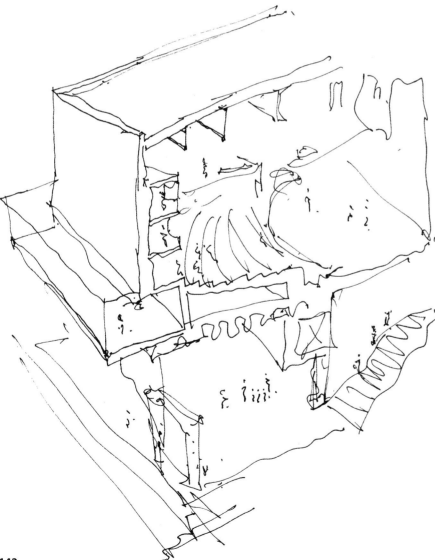

ages attending." Williams eventually arrived at a fully flexible solution based on a series of linked banquettes with no arms or seat numbers.

Williams has challenged normal expectations with the structure, using no columns and featuring a dramatic cantilever over the foyer and pavement. "Normal rules suggest you don't have a big mass supported on light stuff, but heavy at the base, getting lighter. We have turned this on its head, creating tension." This philosophy is even reflected in the finishes, a combination of rough and beautiful raw concrete with finer materials. "Theatre is challenging in many ways to children and we wanted the architecture to be an echo of that. We had never intended it to be 'childlike' but more sculptural."

Client
Unicorn Children's Centre
Capacity
340 (main auditorium)
120 (studio space)
Area
3600 sq. m/38,700 sq. ft
Cost
£13.7m/$25m/€20.6m

WALKER ART CENTER
HERZOG & DE MEURON
MISSOURI, USA 2005

Minneapolis essentially has no street life, partly because of its cold climate and partly because of its system of elevated pedestrian walkways. When Herzog & de Meuron (HDM) embarked on the design for expanding the city's main cultural venue, the Walker Art Center, they set about redressing this, aiming to create a cultural focus – like an artificial town square – to "enhance urban life".

An older theatre on the site was demolished to make way for a sculpture garden, under which (as would be expected in the USA) ample car parking is provided for some 650 cars. HDM's tower housing the new auditorium complements the existing tower built by Edward Barnes in 1971, and doubles the amount of space in the centre. The new building contains extra galleries, offices, a shop, a restaurant and a large 'event' space, as well as a theatre with a fly tower 14.5 m (48 ft) high. It makes a clear statement, neither attempting to match the earlier tower nor to hide itself away, and is positioned to create a visual link with the downtown skyline. The architects explain

that it is "essential not only as an urban landmark: it also expresses the increased importance of the performing arts in the Walker Art Center programme. Inside [is] a theatre encased in a balcony-like, three-storey zone for the audience, somewhat like a downsized version of La Scala in Milan or the open-air Globe Theatre of Shakespeare's day. This audience zone can be used as an exhibition area for all kinds of art installations. Pictorial and performing arts can be interwoven here in entirely unexpected and innovative ways."

The striking exterior features aluminium cladding and irregularly shaped 'slash' windows. The cladding consists of boxes 115 cm (45 in.) square and 20 cm (8 in.) deep, made of aluminium sheeting 5 mm ($^3/_{16}$ in.) thick, in which diamond-shaped perforations have been cut. The result is an almost shimmering skin that changes subtly in different lights. The windows – three huge polygons and various smaller hexags – allow views out from different locations inside the building. As the architects explain, there is logic behind their

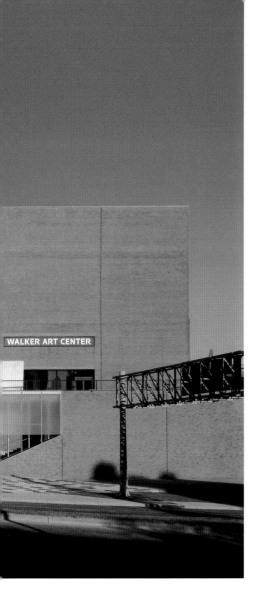

Left: The Art Center is housed in a gleaming, aluminium-clad box, which is linked to the older, brick building by a glass passageway.

Right: At night the glazed areas come to the fore, and lighting brings out the unusual texture of the aluminium cladding.

Bottom right: The front of the theatre volume cantilevers over the street.

seemingly accidental arrangement: "They are homologous forms, showing a kinship in value and structure, somewhat like the shapes of silhouette cutting." The cladding of each box is embossed with a pattern of folds, giving the façade a papery appearance, an effect that HDM have also used inside the theatre. (Interestingly, the architects' De Young Museum in San Francisco, unveiled to much fanfare during the Walker's design and construction process, also has an unusual 'skin', and its form is broadly similar to that of this project.)

The existing brick tower has stood the test of time, and its plain terrazzo floors have both provided curatorial freedom and survived years of heavy foot traffic. Learning from this, HDM have paid special attention to the connection between the two wings and also to visitor orientation, an important but often overlooked element that at worst can detract from visitors' enjoyment and at best simply goes unnoticed. They wanted to achieve a "blend of energies" at street level. Playing on the contrast between the new tower and the older, solid brick form, a fully glazed linking structure allows direct views through the new interior to the sculpture garden. This area is central to the architects' plan for a 'town square' where people can gather without having to go to an exhibition or event. Their intention here is clearly to break down perceived (or real) exclusivity and to create an air of informality that will ultimately tempt more people to participate.

Inside the auditorium, dark colours prevail to produce a strongly 'gothic' atmosphere. The walls are lined with metal embossed with stylized plant motifs, apparently inspired by a piece of lace, and black leather also features. The configuration is essentially rectangular, with classic raked seating, and two rows of balconies at the side and one at high level at the rear. The theatre is equipped with huge technological capability and a large stage for the relatively small size of the auditorium, so that ambitious performances can be put on in an intimate setting.

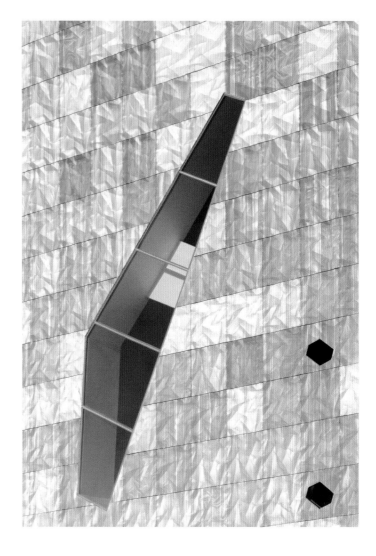

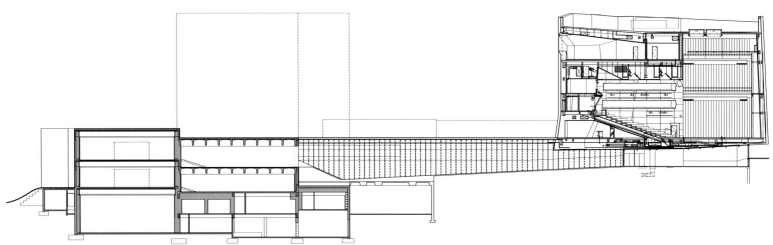

Opposite, top left: The new building contrasts with the original brick tower, without overwhelming it.

Opposite, top right: Irregular windows are cut out of the cladding.

Opposite bottom: The two volumes have been carefully linked with a glazed passageway.

Left: The 'gothic' auditorium features black leather, and its walls echo the patterned aluminium cladding on the outside of the building.

Bottom left and far left: Views out of and through the building have been carefully planned by the arrangement of the seemingly random windows and spaces.

Client
Walker Art Center
Capacity
385
Area
12,000 sq. m/130,000 sq. ft
Cost
£80m/$146m/€ 120m

Libeskind's creations are always driven by passion and often attempt to harness emotion in some way. His great success with the Jewish Museum in Berlin has since been overshadowed somewhat by the fiasco surrounding his design for the site of the World Trade Center in New York. His emotional response to the call for proposals won the competition (run by the city) but failed to deliver the required commercial space for the site owner, who ultimately had to make the project viable.

With this, his first project in Israel, built with associate architects The Heder Partnership (based in Tel Aviv) and funded by the Maurice and Vivienne Wohl Charitable Foundation, Libeskind attempts to express a relationship between knowledge and faith: "Voices and its Echoes [Libeskind's name for the project] stands for the focal point which brings together the two essential components of the Bar-Ilan University: the secular and the sacred. Apparent in the form of the building is the interrelation between the dynamics of knowledge and the unifying role of faith."

The project is located on a crescent-shaped plot on the new 27.5-ha (68-acre) north campus, to the north-east of the central university campus, and is surrounded on all sides by roads. "The building stands on a critical crossroads in the campus and opens a dialogue between the university and its neighbours. As such, Voices and its Echoes is a gateway and beacon for the students, faculty, guests and public of the twenty-first century."

Libeskind's new creation displays the 'sexy' raking lines and angular forms so popular with his contemporaries such as Zaha Hadid and Rem Koolhaas. Flanked by palm trees, it represents a brave design when viewed against a clear blue sky with a distant backdrop of classic white 'block' architecture. The exterior bronze cladding has slot windows in the shape of letters, a feature clearly evolved from the window 'slices' of his Berlin museum. "The exciting forms of the auditorium, lobbies, seminar rooms and public spaces are penetrated by a 'labyrinth of letters' in which an ancient constellation of hierarchies is made visible." Libeskind manipulates the spaces, their functions and the more subtle quality of light to produce an atmosphere that is at once dynamic and meditative.

The visitor enters through a lobby that can be divided into two areas and acts as the spatial hub of the building. The seminar rooms open off this space, and it also has dining and reception areas for public functions, bringing another focus to the complex. The auditorium is sculpted to resemble a 'valley' as an intimate space for visitors listening to a speaker or watching a

THE WOHL CENTRE, BAR-ILAN UNIVERSITY
DANIEL LIBESKIND
RAMAT-GAN, ISRAEL 2005

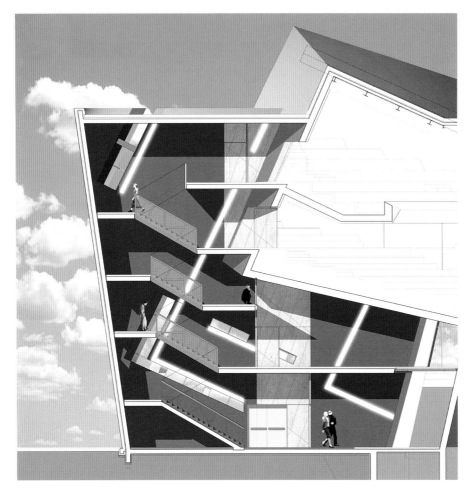

Opposite bottom: The interlocking volumes in the building's exterior continue in the section, and their logic is carried through in the placement of the windows.

Above: The bird-like nature of the concept sketch resurfaces in the finished building, which appears merely to be perching on its site.

performance, and can be configured in a number of ways, providing vital flexibility to accommodate varying audience numbers and simultaneous events. As Libeskind explains, this adaptability is key to his vision for the complex, but is complemented by the exterior's organizing principle: "The entire building functions as a dynamic ensemble which through its flexibility can function equally intensively during the day or the night. The building's exterior is homogeneous in form, built in stone and metal, penetrated by the projections of the labyrinth of letters which defines and organizes the glazing and indirect light."

Viewed from outside, the building is a mass of angles and seemingly disordered shapes, but in plan the central rectangular block that runs through the centre can be seen. On top of this block is a roof terrace. One of the larger rectangular boxes houses the auditorium, which extends in a massive cantilever. When seen from the north, the underside of the cantilever betrays the form of the auditorium floor and gives a tantalizing hint of the seating rows extending down to the stage in the bowels of the building.

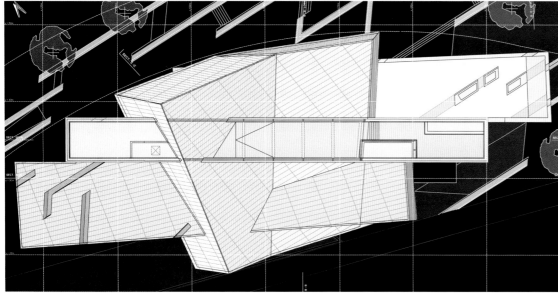

Top and centre: The auditorium is housed in an almost regular rectangular volume tilted on its side; but the real unifying element of the plan is the central block, which runs the full length.

Bottom: The auditorium under construction. The form of the raked seating is echoed outside, in the underside of the cantilevered theatre box.

Opposite: Characteristic Libeskind window-slots pierce the bronze envelope.

Client
Bar-Ilan University donor:
Maurice Wohl Foundation
Capacity
910
Area
3,500 sq. m/37,700 sq. ft
Cost
£3m/$5.5m/€4.5m

SEXTIUS-MIRABEAU THEATRE
GREGOTTI ASSOCIATI INTERNATIONAL
AIX-EN-PROVENCE, FRANCE 2006

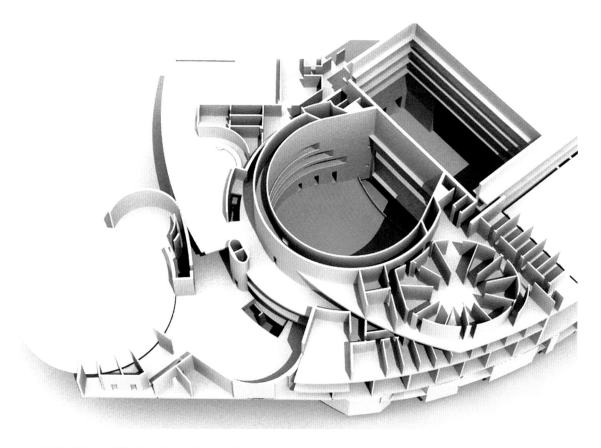

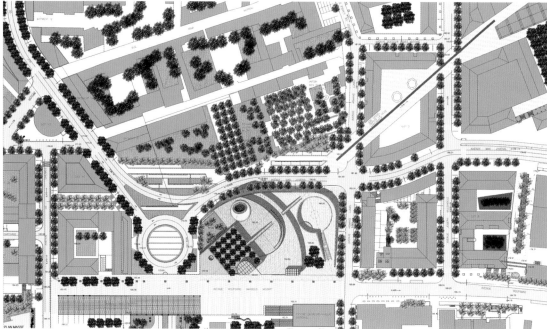

Having recently completed Italy's largest opera house, the Arcimboldi Opera Theatre in Milan (pp. 52–55), which hosted the prestigious La Scala programme during that legendary building's renovation, Gregotti Associati were well qualified to take on this smaller project in the South of France. The new theatre will be used primarily for opera and classical music, and as the venue for the city's musical season as well as for the annual summer festival.

A masterplan previously drawn up by MBM Arquitectes had defined certain geographical constraints for the development. In particular, a new plaza was to be created to function both as the point of entry to the new theatre and as an outdoor theatre space. Vittorio Gregotti realized the significance of this element of the scheme and created a circular plaza, using it as a point of reference for his theatre in the form of a spiralling, circular fort. Gregotti's understanding of the key issues and his basing the design on them may well have been the reasons why he was awarded the job, beating stiff international competition and five other finalists.

He explains his design philosophy: "The theatre is characterized by being grafted on to the site, which itself is a design material because of its differences in height. … The theatre is transformed into a strong landscape figure, which rises up like a terraced hill covered in pale stone. The obvious torsion of the volumes is connected to the curvilinear course of the adjacent road. Thus a succession of lines and circular masses is created; these rise up from the Max Juvénal roundabout in the curved profile of the theatre volume, are reflected in further altimetric variations, and gradually descend into the lowered circular plaza to the side of Avenue Armand Lunel."

The configuration of the theatre elements is also heavily influenced by the circular theme. The elevations and cross-sections provide a deceptive vision of a rectilinear form, but the cutaway model looks more like a mechanical pump, filled with intermeshing cogs and rotors. On plan, the auditorium is easily legible as the hub around which the ancillary workings of the theatre machine are placed, and from the ground, too, its form is clearly identifiable among the ramps, stairs and public spaces.

The importance given to the provision of public spaces and external viewpoints will no doubt help the acceptance of the theatre within the community and to diffuse objections from those who see opera as élitist. Inside, Gregotti has given great importance to circulation, using his geometric configuration to good effect.

The auditorium has three 'inset' balconies providing an additional 400 seats over the main stalls. Red upholstery complements the warm brown of the surrounding walls.

As if to crown his castle, Gregotti has created a large roof terrace, planted with trees and complete with café, on the top of the stage tower, at the highest point in the complex. Possibly the only rectangular space on the site, it offers an imposing viewpoint. The architect explains the thinking behind this part of the building:

"In this way the 'hill' of the theatre becomes a belvedere that looks out on to the surrounding area and becomes an urban icon, a counterpoint to Mont Saint Victoire, the famous mountain with strong geometric volumes immortalized in Cézanne's paintings."

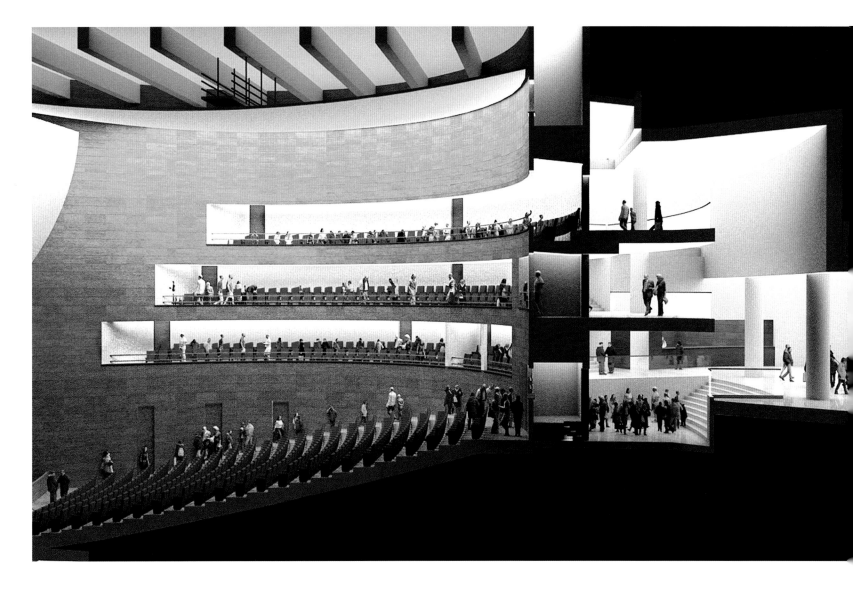

Opposite top: The horseshoe-shaped auditorium is at the centre of the complex.

Opposite bottom: General plan of the area. The roundabout (in blue) is balanced at the opposite side of the site by a circular plaza.

Above: Inset balconies greatly add to the auditorium's capacity.

The building creates its own hill, and is crowned by a viewing terrace. Raised circulation ramps surround the circular plaza at the lowest level.

Client
Communaute du Pays
d'Aix – SEMEPA
Capacity
1300
Area
6000 sq. m/64,500 sq. ft
Cost
£15.7m/$29m/€23m

155

TORREVIEJA MUNICIPAL THEATRE
FOREIGN OFFICE ARCHITECTS
TORREVIEJA, SPAIN 2006

The collaboration of the Spaniard Alejandro Zaera-Polo with the Iranian Farshid Moussavi, the husband-and-wife team who founded Foreign Office Architects (FOA), could be expected to produce some exciting architecture, and their work does not disappoint. After graduating from Harvard University, they were employed in different architectural offices – Moussavi by Renzo Piano and Zaera-Polo by Rafael Moneo – before working together under architectural guru Rem Koolhaas and the

Office for Metropolitan Architecture in Rotterdam in 1991. In 1992 they established FOA in London. Their international portfolio has expanded dramatically in the last ten years, and they have projects in major cities around the world, including Florence, Barcelona, London, Amsterdam, Seoul, Toronto and Yokohama. The scale of their work has also escalated, culminating in their recent appointment to prepare the masterplan for the 2012 Olympic Stadium in London.

One of the major tourist towns in south-east Spain, Torrevieja wanted to raise its profile above the 'mass market' to remain in step with the changing demands of tourists. Visitor numbers were dwindling, and by the turn of the millennium those who did come were looking for more than just reliable sunshine and a sandy beach. The city therefore initiated an ambitious programme of infrastructural improvements in which the new theatre plays an important part.

Below: The longitudinal section shows how the spaces fit together. Ramps on the ground floor lead down to the café and up to the auditorium.

Opposite, top: The cantilevered auditorium forms the ceiling of the foyer, allowing column-free glass walls for the foyer.

Opposite, bottom: Inside, the most striking feature is the auditorium ceiling with its angled, reflective surfaces.

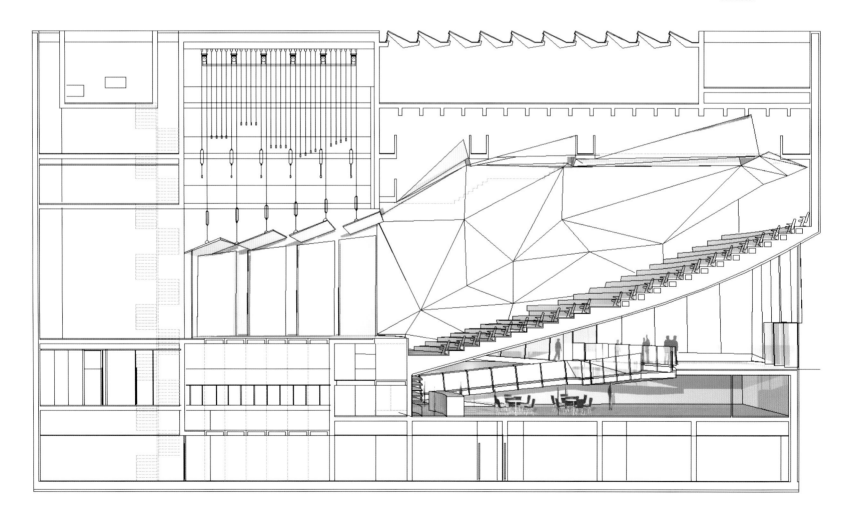

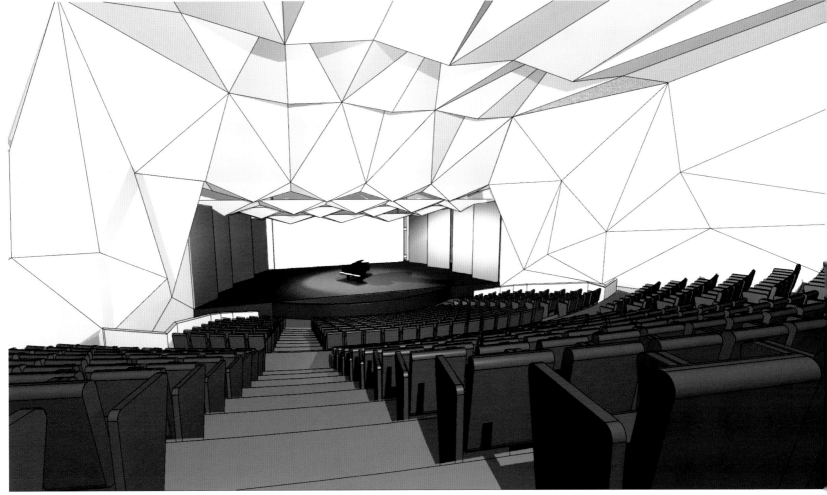

This page: Every space in this tight urban plot is used. The café nestles underneath the 'belly' of the auditorium.

Opposite top: The cross-section reveals two levels of underground car parking.

Opposite bottom: The limestone façade incorporates carved lettering.

The site for the new complex was in an urban block, constrained on all sides and very limited in size. FOA had to use all their creative energy to produce an innovative solution. Rising to the challenge, the architects planned to "lift the auditorium from ground level, letting the plaza penetrate the plot, becoming a foyer that sits underneath the cantilevered mass of the building". This public space would then become "an incision into a solid mass".

Challenges of this type, involving the use of tight urban sites and the conversion of existing spaces, are set to become more frequent for architects. The conversion of a Victorian church in Scotland into the Eastgate Theatre and Arts Centre (pp. 98–101) and the Unicorn Theatre for Children in London (pp. 140–43) both demonstrate that creativity and innovation can produce exciting venues within these constraints. The Torrevieja design has made the most of every space, taking up the full footprint of the site and providing five levels. "The theatre will become a single black box with the scenic tower, in order to allow for the maximum flexibility of use", say the architects. Flexibility is certainly a key element of this project, as in any theatre with restricted space, and one example of it is the non-structural proscenium that can be dismantled to widen the performance area.

The design resembles a 'curled up' shoebox, and its refreshingly simple shape instantly betrays the line of the auditorium seating inside. It could well become the definitive form for auditoria with limited space. Every inch of available room is used to fit in the specified 650 seats. The auditorium is configured in the 'classic' rectangular format for safe acoustic performance, with a single rake for the seating, which is arranged in a gentle arc. The foyer is at ground level; below that is a café-style bar, and two levels of car parking are located below the plaza. The building envelope is made up of reinforced-concrete walls 400-mm (15¾-in.) thick, cast in-situ, with smaller beams forming the auditorium ceiling.

The exterior of the theatre is clad in local limestone to match that of the rest of the block, and includes the almost obligatory lettering on the façade – a device also seen on the Wales Millennium Centre (pp. 112–15), Jakob + MacFarlane's Fanal Theatre in France (pp. 160–63) and RMJM's planned Theatre Royal in Dumfries, Scotland.

The successful completion of this small 'packaged' theatre in Spain no doubt enhanced the practice's portfolio, and may well have aided their successful bid for the prestigious Music Box project for the BBC in London's White City (pp. 230–33).

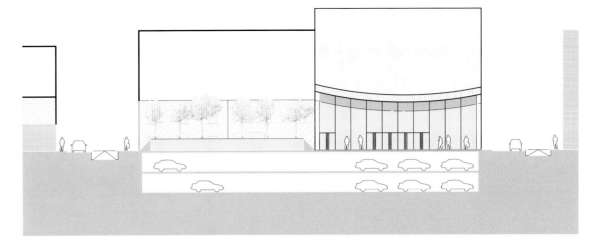

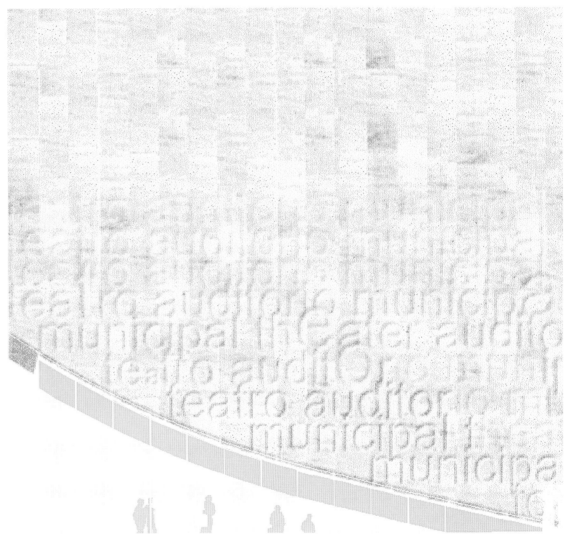

Client
Town of Torrevieja

Capacity
650

Area
Not available

Cost
Not available

FANAL THEATRE
JAKOB + MACFARLANE
SAINT-NAZAIRE, FRANCE 2007

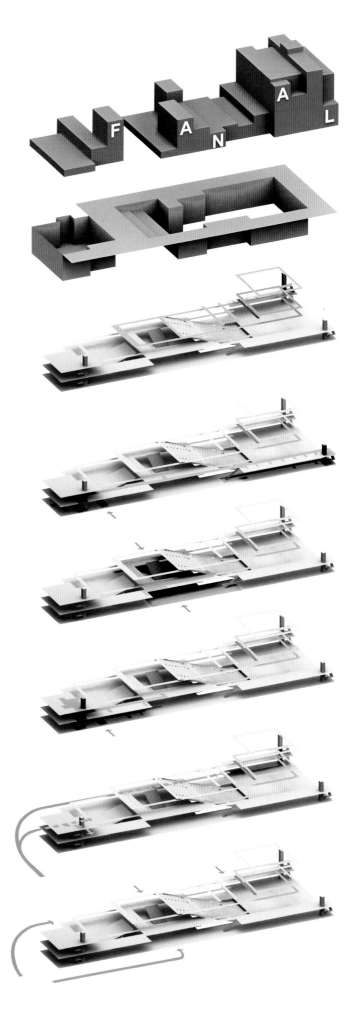

As proof of chaos theory, the origins of Jakob + MacFarlane's Fanal Theatre can be traced back to an event in 1942. The mighty German battleship *Tirpitz* was holed up in a Norwegian fjord, and the British, desperate to deprive the fearsome ship of a dry dock (which would have enabled it to operate in the Atlantic), sought to destroy the only such facilities at the strategic French port of Saint-Nazaire, at the mouth of the Loire. The massive raids also damaged key infrastructure, including the harbour's railway station.

In the early twentieth century, the railway station was often the focal point of a town, the hub of its comings and goings. Saint-Nazaire's life-blood was the port and the railway network that linked it to the rest of France. The city has grown in the decades since the Second World War; the port is now a major centre for the container industry and trucks have largely taken over from trains, but the town and its inhabitants have turned their backs on this area. Paris-based practice Jakob + MacFarlane had the task of re-establishing the historic focus of Saint-Nazaire, not with a new station but with a cultural icon: the remains of the station building were to be used as an important part of an adventurous regeneration plan involving the creation of a new theatre. The town's mayor, Joël Batteux, is behind an ambitious scheme to turn the town back towards the sea, thereby reminding its citizens that the port is the reason for Saint-Nazaire's existence.

In homage to the station's heritage, the new structure stands entirely within the footprint of the original building. According to their design statement, the architects set out to "take the existing building grid of 4.5 × 4.5 m (15 × 15 ft) and from this produce a new conceptual grid that is extruded upwards and downwards to different heights in order to meet the varying functional and spatial needs … of each part of the programme".

The architects further explain their logic as a "new kind of extruded topographic language, of solidity and transparency". The strongly cubic form of the building makes a clear reference to the nearby container port, but its boxy extrusions also provide the volume necessary for the machinery above stage. The distinctive addition to the town's skyline is further signalled by enormous letters spelling out the theatre's name. The architects have

successfully embedded the fingerprints of the past within the contemporary narrative: the shape, massing, footprint and orientation of the station are still readable, but the design is obviously new. The building is divided into three parts: a main theatre; a rehearsal theatre and artists' accommodation with administration rooms; and the entrance and exhibition hall, workshop and café.

Inside, the theatre does not disappoint. One exterior elevation has been re-formed in glass, providing a light and airy entrance and foyer with exposed walkways and balconies threading through the space at different levels. Essential to the experience of the theatre's interior is its ability to provide two theatre layouts: it can be set up either as an open thrust-stage arrangement, called the "storm" by the architects, or as a more traditional proscenium layout, in which the audience and the stage are segregated. The auditorium is particularly original, drawing on the classic shoebox form but presented in an uncluttered and clearly contemporary fashion. The seating follows a gentle curve and is cut through by two walkways. Each side has two refreshingly simple platform galleries, which, in a complete break from tradition, are linked by a high-level gantry-cum-walkway hanging over the audience. Although the interior is advanced in its technology, it is very simple in appearance and retreats into the background rather than competing with the performance for the audience's attention.

Opposite: Conceptual
models show how the
form and access routes
are planned.

Above: The theatre
emerges out of the old
station building.

Right: The blocky form of
the building is led by the
spaces it contains.

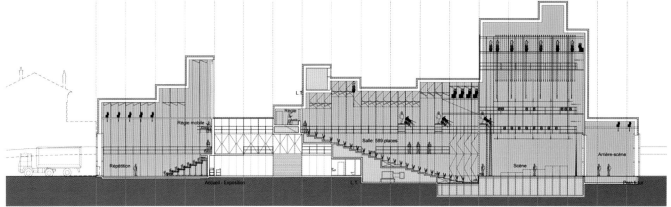

Opposite top: Jakob + MacFarlane have integrated old and new to exciting effect.

Opposite bottom: The fully glazed foyer creates a light and transparent interior.

Above: An unusual feature of the auditorium is the high-level gantry crossing the stalls.

Client
Town of Saint-Nazaire
Capacity
600
Area
4600 sq. m/50,000 sq. ft
Cost
Not available

The new theatre in Lelystad forms a key part of a masterplan for the city centre drawn up by urban design and landscape architecture firm West 8. The brief for the theatre required it to "play an important role providing a cluster of cultural and social activities in this new quarter that would give Lelystad an active cultural life". As the project has unfolded, the typology of the multi-functional theatre has become ever more complex, but the architects, UN Studio, have striven to harness this into a flexible, transparent and intelligent design.

The architects explain the logic behind the new building in its urban setting: "The theatre forms an important orientation point with a forthright architectonical look. Approached from the central station, the theatre tower is a striking accent in the skyline. At night the volume is lit up, and easily visible from the different parking facilities."

At first sight, two overpowering elements strike the viewer. The first is the theatre's form, with its raking lines reminiscent of the work of Zaha Hadid; the second is the brave use of orange. Each individual plane is a different hue, enhancing the shadows and angular forms, and the architects have used plenty of creative thinking to integrate some excellent features into these angles and shapes. The north façade is particularly interesting, with the space under the great raking cantilever of the theatre mass creating a glazed 'underbelly'. This device, also used by Foreign Office Architects in their Torrevieja Municipal Theatre (pp. 156–59), is an effective way of challenging the visitor's subconscious expectations of conventional building forms.

The architects have also created a spectacular gallery/balcony on the first floor. In an excellent example of a fully considered design, the cave-like orifice is fully integrated into the elevation. The architects explain further: "The interaction between different art disciplines should be integrated in the design process of these buildings. UN Studio's expertise lies in an analytical approach to the design requirements. During the research process, before the design begins, questions regarding special organization and the multi-functional use of the theatre have an important role."

AGORA THEATRE
UN STUDIO
LELYSTAD, THE NETHERLANDS 2007

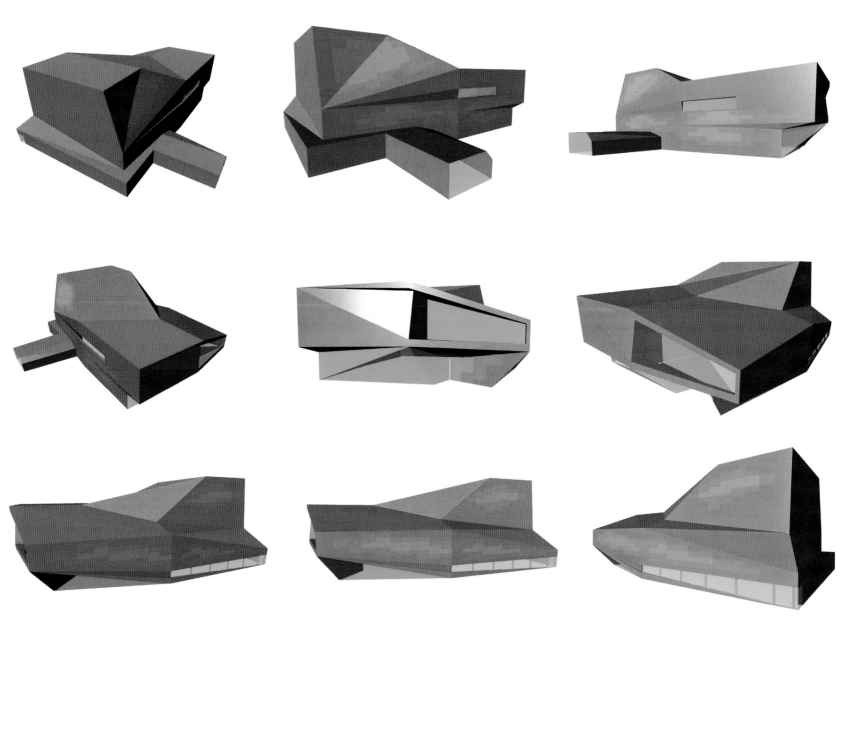

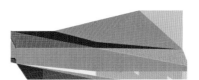

Renderings showing
the development of the
building's form (opposite;
top and middle) and the
colour treatment of the
façade (above).

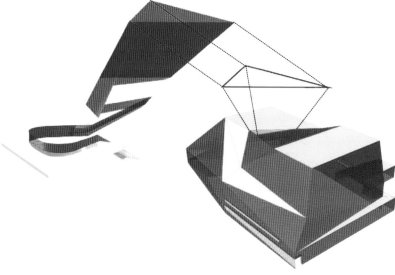

Above: The main entrance. The balcony provides views over the public area to the front of the theatre.

Left: Rendering of the building's form

Opposite: The extraordinary sculptural treatment does not stop at the exterior. The foyer and circulation are just as spectacular.

Inside the building, the visual impact is equally strong. The straight lines of the exterior are replaced here with great sweeping, sculptural forms enhanced again by the use of bright colours on the stairs and balcony sides, in strong contrast to the pure white of the other surfaces.

The architects have skilfully raised the visitor's expectations with their treatment of the lobbies and circulation spaces, building anticipation of the performing space itself. Suitably, the auditorium provides the climax of this fantastic sculptural setting. However, the incorporation of such a bright colour in this context, though clearly creating the required impact, must be questioned. It is surely a distraction, particularly for the performers; and the forms of the balconies and the auditorium envelope are so stunning in themselves that they could no doubt produce the same effect without the steroid colours.

Behind all the arresting colour and sculpture, though, is a layout that is surprisingly clearly structured and logically ordered. The ground floor contains the Grand Café, set in a triangular lobby area flanked by the vast glazed elevation and bounded by the stairs to the upper level and the main auditorium. The first floor houses the smaller, 200-seat 'box' theatre with its own foyer and three multi-functional rooms around the perimeter. Here, the all-important bar is, like the café below, set against the glazed elevation, and engages with the public areas at the front of the theatre.

The staggering use of colour in the auditorium has produced a space that is a performer in its own right.

Client
Municipality of Lelystad
Capacity
725 (big hall)
200 (small hall)
Area
7000 sq. m/75,300 sq. ft
Cost
£8.5m/$15.6m/€12.4m

ROYAL FESTIVAL HALL
ALLIES AND MORRISON
LONDON, UK 1951/2007

The Royal Festival Hall (RFH) on the south bank of London's River Thames is important not only as the first Modern public building in the UK but also as one of the most significant examples of early post-war buildings in Britain. Few large concert halls had been built in the first half of the twentieth century, and the RFH represented an early application of great advances in technology in a major performing venue.

The RFH was designed by London County Council's Architects' Department for the 1951 Festival of Britain, and provides a fascinating insight into the optimistic era in which it was built. Its architectural success, however, was undermined by poor acoustics, and fundamental errors in design have dogged the hall since its opening. History has shown that acoustic technology had not evolved far enough at the time the RFH was built. Engineers had grasped the basics of acoustic principles and understood the characteristics required for a fine concert space, but they lacked the sheer wealth of data required to apply the principles to a specific design. One element in particular proved problematic. Engineers knew that sound was absorbed by the

audience and had duly estimated an absorption coefficient of 0.33 per person (1 being full absorption and 0 being full reflection); but modern-day acousticians have found that 0.57 is the correct figure. This error resulted in the catastrophic undersizing of the hall, creating a reverberation time of a mere 1.5 seconds, far short of the desired 2.2 seconds. The direct relationship between the number of seats and the volume of a space has now become the fundamental principle in the design of any performing venue.

The building suffered a series of 'improvements' over the next few decades, but it was not until 1987 that acoustic engineers Kirkegaard Associates were commissioned to assess the concert hall for a major overhaul. They started to collect comprehensive performance data, both by taking measurements and by working with the orchestra. In 1993, Kirkegaard was engaged to develop acoustic recommendations for the much-needed restoration and remodelling of the hall. These recommendations were developed further with the aid of computer testing and modelling and later with acoustic

testing of $\frac{1}{16}$-size models. The baseline data obtained was used to calibrate all subsequent design changes.

Unsurprisingly, the analysis showed that no single change in the hall would have enough effect on the acoustics. An extensive remodelling necessitated a close collaboration between Kirkegaard and Allies and Morrison to maintain the architectural integrity of the hall while transforming it to achieve the acoustic, technical and functional goals.

The work includes narrowing and deepening the platform to improve sight-lines among the orchestra members and to increase acoustic support for the performers. The organ is moved back by 1.2 m (4 ft); this is no mean feat but will have a significant effect on the performance both of the hall and of the instrument. The timber canopy above the platform has been replaced by lightweight tensioned fabric with a new timber-clad concrete ceiling above it. The ceiling and canopy are designed to provide a rich and precise response from the space for the performers. The specially designed fabric will provide gentle sound reflections to support ensemble playing, while allowing mid- and low-frequency sound to pass through to the heavy ceiling to create warmth and fullness. The fabric reflectors will be backlit to give them a soft glow.

To recapture the building's integrity, Allies and Morrison have had to unravel some of the work previously carried out. They have reinstated the prominence of the 1951 circulation routes, but have incorporated modern requirements for increased accessibility, including new lifts. The entrances are better defined and the concrete balustrades that have hemmed in the building since the 1960s have been removed – a small but vital element of this ambitious refurbishment – to invite in a new generation of concert-goers.

Left: The revamp of the Festival Hall will inject new life into the popular South Bank area. It is part of a larger scheme to improve this section of the riverside, including the installation of lighting, the planting of trees and the encourage-ment of new businesses.

Top: The auditorium following its refurbish-ment. The hall has always been difficult to play in, and the tensioned fabric canopy will improve the experience for the performers.

Above: Before work began, the auditorium featured a timber canopy over the stage.

Client
South Bank Centre
Capacity
2900
Area
1,700 sq. m/18,500 sq. ft
Cost
£91m/$167.6m/€133m

EXPERIMENTAL MEDIA AND PERFORMING ARTS CENTER
GRIMSHAW
TROY, NY, USA 2007

The devil is in the brief. So say many architects who receive imprecise commissions. "Never mind the detail; we must agree on what we are building first." The number of projects that begin despite fundamental misconceptions about the finished article is astonishing: the theatre within Paul Andreu's Oriental Art Centre in Shanghai, for example, became an opera hall in a single telephone call (pp. 90–93); and nothing can eclipse Henning Larsens Tegnestue's Copenhagen Opera (pp. 94–97), which was defined when the architects were engaged only as a "public building".

After Nicholas Grimshaw (working with acoustician Kirkegaard Associates) was commissioned in 2001 to design a 1200-seat multi-purpose hall and a 500-seat recital hall for an upstate New York university, the brief was changed and subsequently required a 1200-seat concert hall and a 400-seat theatre with fly tower. Furthermore, the main hall had to be optimized for symphonic concerts but capable of accommodating film, jazz and some types of dance. The project was also to include two black-box studios, a rehearsal stage, a radio station, audio and video suites, studios for artists in residence,

and classrooms. So different are the requirements that such an alteration is the equivalent of changing a brief for a school to one for a hospital.

The brief called for "world-class acoustics", which means NC-15-rated spaces for the two studios, the concert hall and the theatre. Such a low NC (noise control) level signifies negligible background noise and requires an extremely high standard of acoustic isolation for a compact building with so many separate performance spaces. The venues had to be capable of operating at the same time, at full volume, which meant that they had to be structurally independent: in essence four individual buildings inside one large building, either with separate foundations or, in the case of Studio 1, sitting on a network of steel springs. Furthermore, two of the venues had acoustically sensitive accommodation – the radio station and the audio and video suites – stacked on top of them, requiring completely separate steel structures to support respectively the concrete roofs of the venues below and the concrete floors of the rooms above.

The concert hall sits in the main circulation space of the building, towards

the bottom of the sloping site, and is encapsulated in a curved 'hull' of cedar planks. This hull is a prominent feature of the internal space and, illuminated at night, visible through the glass curtain wall on the north façade, is the signature element of the building. Configured in a classic 'shoebox' design, the auditorium is loosely modelled on the tried-and-tested formula of the great nineteenth-century European halls such as Vienna's Musikverein. It has convex walls for acoustic diffusion and a unique curved ceiling made of Nomex. This material reflects high- and mid-frequency sound back to the performers and the audience, for clarity and accurate spatial location of instruments, while letting low-frequency sound pass through to the upper volume of the hall to create reverberation and warmth. This effect is commonly achieved in twentieth-century halls with a suspended canopy above the concert platform, but here the ceiling eliminates the need for such a canopy, making the auditorium less cluttered and more architecturally legible. Walls are in a combination of maple, cast plaster and cast stone, and floors are of maple.

The rectangular south wing, clad in white glass, is a counterpoint to the concert hall and atrium, and contains the theatre, the two studios, all the centre's other performance-related spaces and most of its supporting infrastructure.

The theatre is a very simple rectangular space with a subtle architectural character that recedes completely when the house lights are lowered. In this flexible and audience-friendly hall, a mere 23-cm (9-in.) difference in height between the seats and the stage breaks down the boundary between performer and audience; and the balcony and gallery seats are loose, so that these areas can be occupied by performers (with the audience restricted to the central seating block) or even extended across the stage for an audience-in-the-round configuration. Dark grey plastered walls, black architectural steel, and maple elements such as the seat backs and the balustrade infill panels make up a straightforward palette of materials.

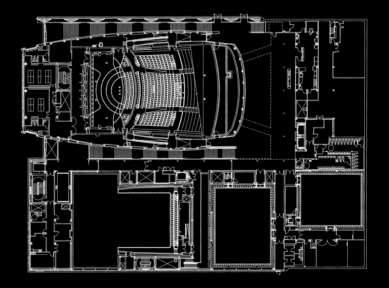

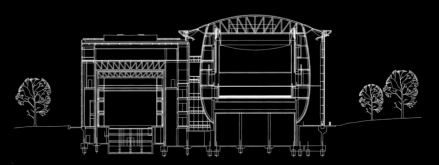

Opposite and above left: The transparent foyer to the east of the site allows views through to the main space, the concert hall in its curved box of cedar wood.

Above right: The north façade is entirely of glass, 30.5 m (100 ft) tall at its highest point.

Left: The independence of the spaces is crucial to the building's acoustic performance.

Bottom left: The north–south section shows the structural separation of the concert hall and theatre.

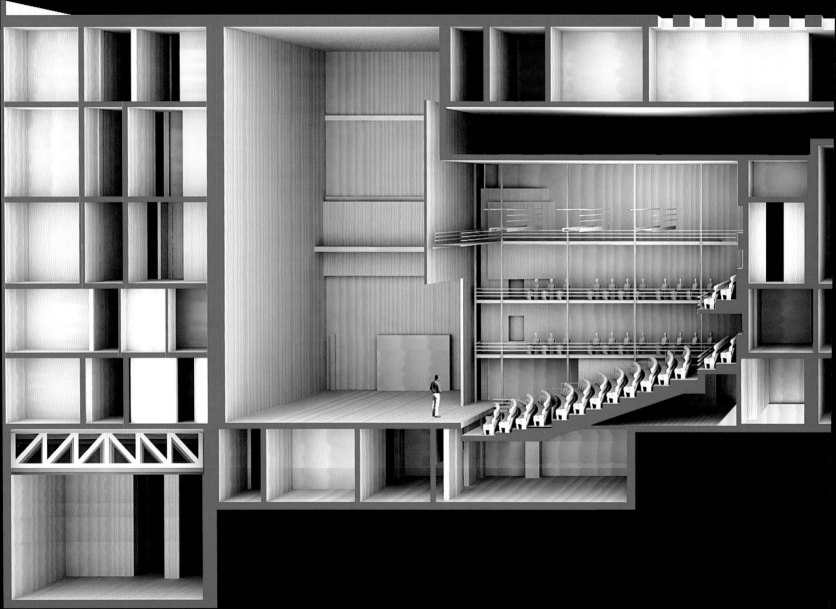

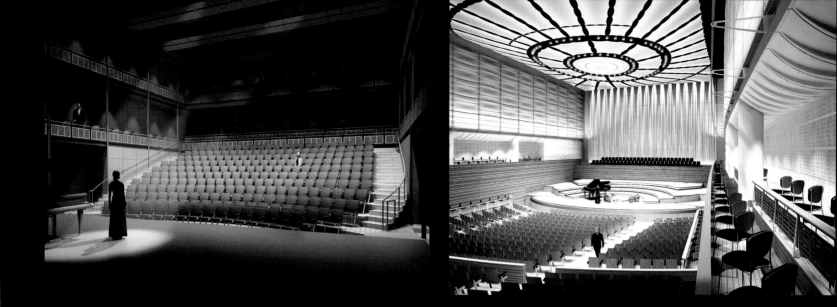

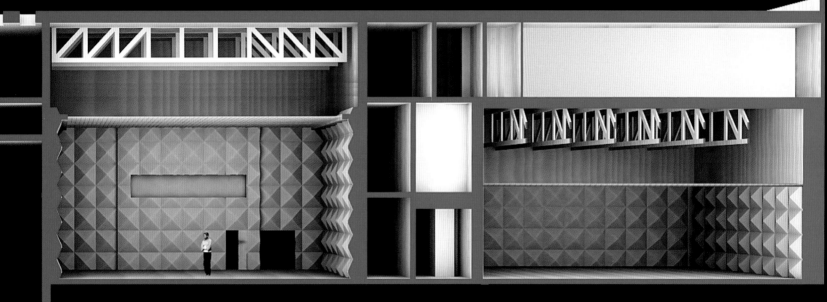

Client
Rensselaer Polytechnic
Institute
Capacity
1200 (concert hall)
400 (theatre)
Area
20,000 sq. m/215,000 sq. ft
Cost
£68.7m/$126.4m/

KING'S PLACE
DIXON JONES
LONDON, UK 2007

This is something of an encore for Dixon Jones, who had been projected into the limelight (literally) with their massive refurbishment of London's Royal Opera House (ROH). With King's Place, they now have a chance to build a performing space from scratch. The ROH was a particularly sensitive and public project, and involved pressure from all sides, not only architectural – they were, in effect, ripping apart a national icon – but also from others, not least the opera company that was losing revenue during the work. The project was taking so long that the management actually became concerned that their ageing audience had developed other loyalties and might be lost forever. They need not have worried. The result has been widely acknowledged as a success, and the house is even more spectacular and popular than ever.

It was, therefore, inevitable that Dixon Jones would be expected to perform again, and use their hard-won experience on another auditorium. King's Place is very different to the ROH, of course. It is interesting as an example of inner-city regeneration, and involves all the typical challenges of working within an existing streetscape and the commercial demands of funding cultural activities. The block has a constrained footprint, and replaces warehouses and a public house backing on to a canal, just north of the centre of London. It is fully mixed-use – and revenue from the 26,000 sq. m (280,000 sq. ft) of office space will no doubt fund the music venue. The five floors of offices dominate the street-scape at the front of the building, and at the rear a seven-storey circular tower, with a brasserie at ground level, overlooks the Battlebridge canal basin. Next to the tower, a rectangular block containing a formal restaurant lines the south bank of the canal. Opposite is the site of the new Channel Tunnel rail terminal, but the area is currently barren and greatly in need of humanizing development such as this project.

The entrance is from York Way through the west elevation and leads into a public atrium, where the mixed-use nature of the development really becomes obvious. To the right there are a sculpture gallery, WCs, access to the restaurant, and the reception area for the offices. To the left are the concert-hall box office, stairs to the upper level and access to the brasserie. These diverse facilities do not allow much scope for creating an impact specifically for concert-goers, but they do show how the constraints of tight urban sites can be appropriately managed.

The auditorium is of safe 'shoebox' configuration with classic raked seating leading down to the stage. Designed mainly for small chamber-music recitals, it can also accommodate larger ensembles if necessary. A variable absorption curtain 6 m (20 ft) deep can be drawn horizontally around the entire perimeter of the upper half of the hall, behind columns, to adjust the acoustic of the room and make it more suited to jazz, world music and other types of performance needing amplified sound.

This project, while at the opposite end of the scale from the work at the ROH, is particularly interesting as an exemplar of how it will be possible to integrate cultural venues into tight urban sites when space is at an even higher premium. Keith Williams' Unicorn Theatre for Children (pp. 140–43) is another example, and, although that project is aimed at a younger audience, the compact footprint presented similar challenges. The mixed-use aspect of King's Place is also of note. One of London's rare 1960s successes has been the highly acclaimed Barbican Centre by Chamberlin, Powell & Bon, which contains housing, a concert hall, galleries and restaurants. The Dixon Jones project, as a smaller version of the Barbican model, is one to be watched; but as the construction contract is being run by the client on a 'design and build' basis, the development may well turn out to be more commercial than cultural.

Left: Floor plan (top) and longitudinal section (bottom) of the auditorium. Designed in collaboration with Arup Acoustics, the hall has a fully adjustable acoustic to accommodate larger ensembles, and performances requiring amplified sound.

Opposite: The building's stone angularity is moderated on the west façade with an undulating glass skin that will transform the streetscape. The office floors are supported by columns.

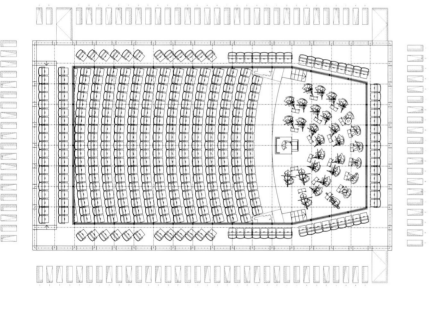

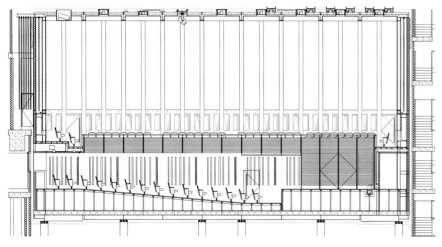

Client
Parabola Land Ltd
Capacity
425
Area
27,500 sq. m/300,000 sq. ft
Cost
£97.8m/$180m/€ 143.2m

LEICESTER THEATRE AND PERFORMING ARTS CENTRE
RAFAEL VIÑOLY ARCHITECTS
LEICESTER, UK 2007

In 2003, Leicester was in decline. In one part of the city, St George's, eighty per cent of the buildings were vacant or under-used, but the quality of the architecture was high, hence the district's designation as a conservation area and its enormous potential for regeneration. Plans included the creation of a cultural quarter as a catalyst for regeneration, to contain a new theatre with two auditoria seating 750 and 350. The City Council, which commissioned the building, believed that theatre was still too élitist and wanted to turn it inside out, breaking down the conventional barriers between actors and audience.

Rafael Viñoly was fascinated by this and saw it as an opportunity to create something radical. He developed his proposal based on this one issue, questioning the traditional role of the theatre head-on. His gamble paid off and he won the commission against stiff competition from established players. Viñoly had toyed with this concept in the Kimmel Center in Philadelphia (pp. 42–47), 'loosening the barrier' between backstage and front of house; at Leicester he was to break it down completely.

Having committed himself to this idea, Viñoly had to deliver. To break down a division reinforced by years of tradition would be to enter new territory, and required some really innovative thinking. Could the two worlds of backstage and front of house really start interacting with and benefiting from each other? Viñoly

wanted the theatre to be transparent, and not elevated in the usual way. He used the street as a reference point so that people could move freely through the theatre as though it were a public plaza.

During the design process Viñoly challenged some of the most fundamental principles of theatre. "Why define the stage as it is? Why not integrate the foyer and stage as one zone? Why not allow the performance to occur on the stage but let it bleed out around the edges to the foyer or even let it move to the street so that the boundaries of the performances are not limited to the theatre itself?" A grid sweeping through the entire complex was to prove the masterstroke that gave Viñoly the flexibility he needed to realize his vision. The grid supports lighting and sound equipment and allows performances to occur anywhere in the building. Sets of sliding curtains can modify the space according to the performance and the availability of natural light. These also function as acoustic curtains and conform to fire-safety regulations, and constitute a reference to the city's strong heritage of textile-making.

The grid successfully blurs the boundaries between the theatre's various elements, lending a unique transparency to the two auditoria, the foyer and the ancillary spaces. Viñoly placed the stage between the two auditoria, because the larger auditorium was expected to use the main stage for the majority of the time but could also be closed off and used as a

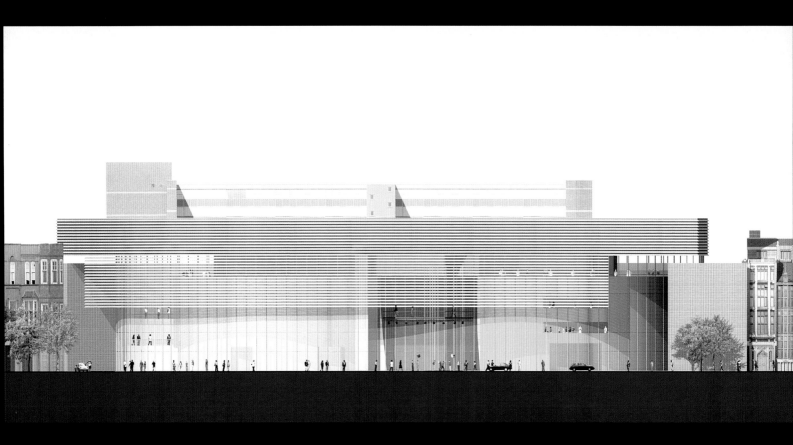

concert hall. This configuration increases the capacity of the smaller auditorium to 450 seats and the realms of possibility expand dramatically.

By this point in the design process, the client had seen the possibilities created by such flexibility and had torn up the programme; they now envisaged four or five performing spaces. The theatre company, however, needed more persuasion. Viñoly worked closely with them and also employed a theatre consultant. After some initial scepticism they saw the opportunities of increased interaction with the audience and started introducing ideas to make the flexibility work for them, pushing the vision still further. These included creating dynamic performance spaces that move around during a show, and moving audiences around during intermissions.

The offices, dressing rooms and workshops are positioned at the perimeter on balconies overlooking the performing space. Usually these ancillary functions are located in different parts of the building and interact very little, but in Viñoly's configuration the foyer becomes a reference point for them. Any activity, such as rigging on the stage, can be seen by people in the dressing rooms and in the restaurant area. This visual connection enables the whole complex to convey a sense of being alive twenty-four hours a day. Viñoly's vision goes further, however – he wants to take the life of the theatre beyond the external walls, exposing intriguing glimpses of stage preparation to the outside and perhaps even persuading passers-by to find out more.

Opposite; top: The centre from the east (opposite) and south (top). Viñoly has created a transparent envelope to break down conventional cultural barriers and make the theatre as inclusive as possible. One of the curtains is seen in purple.

Above: At night, lighting brings the internal volumes to life. The red volume is the smaller auditorium; the main space is to its right.

Client
Leicester City Council
Capacity
750; 350–450
Area
13,000 sq. m/140,000 sq. ft
Cost
Not available

NATIONAL GRAND THEATRE OF CHINA
PAUL ANDREU
BEIJING, CHINA 2007

In the heart of Beijing, just one block from Tiananmen Square and opposite the Forbidden City, this ambitious building is at the centre of China's push to launch its capital on to the world's cultural stage in preparation for the 2008 Olympic Games. For French architect Paul Andreu it was no time for stage fright, no time to melt quietly into the surrounding architecture, but rather the time for bold and brave statements. This is his biggest project to date and one by which he will be judged in years to come. Andreu sums up the challenge: "The decision to build the National Grand Theatre in a place of such historical and symbolic importance clearly testifies to the importance given to culture in its relationship with history and the contemporary world."

It was obvious to Andreu that in this context both an obscure building and an isolated structure were out of the question. He explains his approach: "We strove to create a building that shows respect for the buildings around it (each of which marks in varying degrees the history of architecture in China) but that demonstrates the vitality of modern architecture by being as bold as they were in their day."

The striking result enabled Andreu to fight off some sixty-eight other international architects to win the commission; but the scheme was not without its critics, being dubbed 'the jellyfish' by its detractors. In fact it has been at the centre of a major controversy since its conception. Visually, it could not be more at odds with the local architecture, but by completely surrounding the building with a lake, Andreu has produced an innovative 'buffer' so that his creation is seen in isolation.

The lake forms an important part of the design, as access to the building is limited to a vast underwater tunnel 60 m (200 ft) long. By using this device, Andreu is able to increase the visitor's level of anticipation, first by making the building appear inaccessible from most directions, and secondly by making the entrance an experience in its own right. The tunnel roof is glazed, providing ample natural light, and the space itself is used as an impressive gallery. Andreu explains its function as follows: "This entrance leaves the exterior of the building intact, without any openings, and mysterious-looking, while providing the public with a passage

from their daily world to the world of opera, fiction and dreams."

The building's footprint is 213 × 144 m (700 × 470 ft), and its titanium and glass envelope has a vast surface area of almost 150,000 sq. m (1,600,000 sq. ft), forming a 'super ellipsoid' with a maximum height of some 46 m (151 ft). Despite its name, the National Grand Theatre is in fact a complex of three auditoria (like Andreu's earlier Oriental Art Centre in Shanghai; pp. 90–93): a 2416-seat opera house, 2017-seat concert hall and 1040-seat theatre. As is the case of many of the projects in this book, it is in the areas between the performing spaces that the architect has excelled: rather than simply designing 'utility' areas, he has created vast and exciting spaces that reach up to the underside of the roof. These areas are open to the public and include footways, bridges, balconies, squares, shops, restaurants and cafés. However, even these have attracted criticism, some likening the spaces to airport departure lounges – a clear snipe at Andreu's vast portfolio of fifty international airport projects and his lack of experience in designing cultural destinations.

Andreu's National Theatre will form part of a string of Olympic-driven major projects in Beijing led by Western architects, including Rem Koolhaas/OMA's headquarters for Chinese state television and a stadium by Herzog & de Meuron. This ambitious building programme has itself been a source of controversy, with many complaining that the character of Beijing is changing irrevocably and that the traditional principles of Chinese architecture are being overlooked.

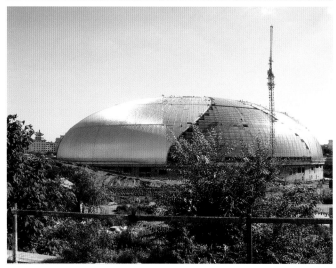

The site is next to the Forbidden City. The building has a strong presence and its curvaceous glass and metal roof is highly visible from all directions.

The lake is intended to
lessen the impact on the
surrounding area. The
complex is entered
through a tunnel, seen
here at lower left.

This page: The project's name belies the variety of performances that can be accommodated. Two of the spaces are the concert hall (top) and the opera house (bottom).

Opposite, top: The cross-section of the main theatre shows the vast underground spaces.

Opposite, bottom: Surrounded by extensive public areas, the concert hall (top), main theatre (centre) and opera theatre (bottom) are entirely separate under the over-arching roof.

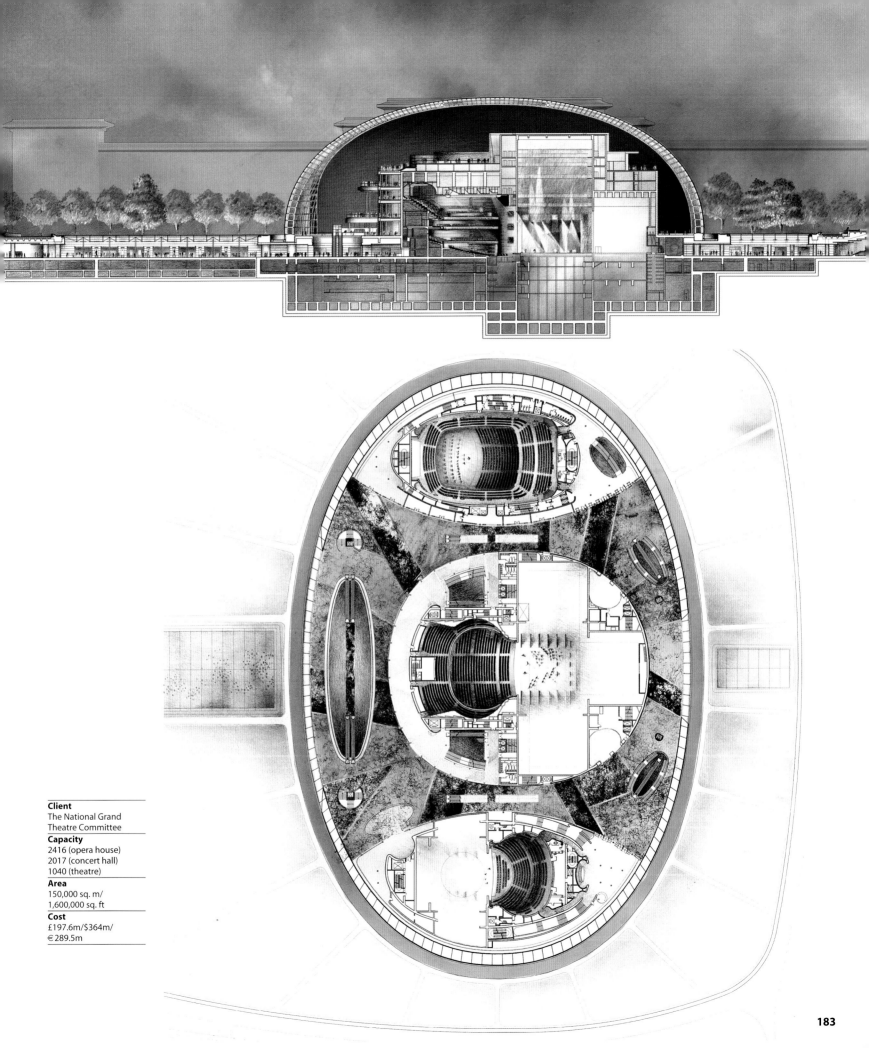

Client
The National Grand
Theatre Committee

Capacity
2416 (opera house)
2017 (concert hall)
1040 (theatre)

Area
150,000 sq. m/
1,600,000 sq. ft

Cost
£197.6m/$364m/
€289.5m

GRAND CANAL PERFORMING ARTS CENTRE AND GALLERIA
DANIEL LIBESKIND
DUBLIN, REPUBLIC OF IRELAND 2008

Amid all the furore of the World Trade Center redevelopment, Daniel Libeskind has been steadily building a portfolio of realized projects. He was initially part of an élite group of highly acclaimed but unbuilt architects (who also included Zaha Hadid). He has now left this behind by completing his moving Jewish Museum in Berlin and the Imperial War Museum North in Manchester, UK, as well as having two performing spaces in design, one of which is the Wohl Centre in Israel (pp. 148–51).

The radical 'distorted rhomboid' form of the Grand Canal Performing Arts Centre with its angular lines is of the Hadid/Koolhaas ilk, and characteristically brave. The theatre creates a focus for a canalside piazza (containing a hotel, apartments and offices) and is flanked by two 'galleria' with retail and office space

and courtyards providing cafés, restaurants and shops. The building's importance is enhanced when it is illuminated at night. The whole complex forms an attractive covered link between the Liffey quayside and the square; and the public space on the waterfront is complemented by the impressive indoor spaces of the gallerias.

Libeskind reveals the rationale of his design: "The concept ... is to build a powerful cultural presence expressed in a dynamic volume. This volume is sculpted to express the various forces which create the urban piazza, the public space and inner workings of the theatre. This composition creates an icon that mirrors the joy and drama emblematic of Dublin itself."

More specifically, Libeskind wanted the Grand Canal project to "enhance the developing urban structure of Grand Canal

Harbour with an exciting public landmark, a magnet for Dublin, a destination for working, shopping, living and entertainment, twenty-four hours a day [and] seven days a week". The design is based on a concept of stages: of the theatre itself, of the piazza and of the terraces that overlook it. The piazza acts as a grand outdoor lobby for the theatre. As Libeskind explains, "with the dramatic theatre elevation as a backdrop and platforms for viewing, the piazza itself becomes a stage for civic gathering".

Libeskind has used a straightforward reinforced-concrete skeleton over a steel sub-structure, with façades of prefabricated modular glass and metal elements. Some of the public areas break daringly through the angled glass to provide balconies cantilevered high above the piazza. Libeskind has clearly matched the design

Opposite: Libeskind's characteristic slashed windows are clearly visible in the concept sketch.

Right: The complex addresses the quay, creating a pleasant public area by the water.

Below: Looking rather like an alien spaceship, the building's spectacular frontage draws people in. The cantilevered balconies are visible above the entrance.

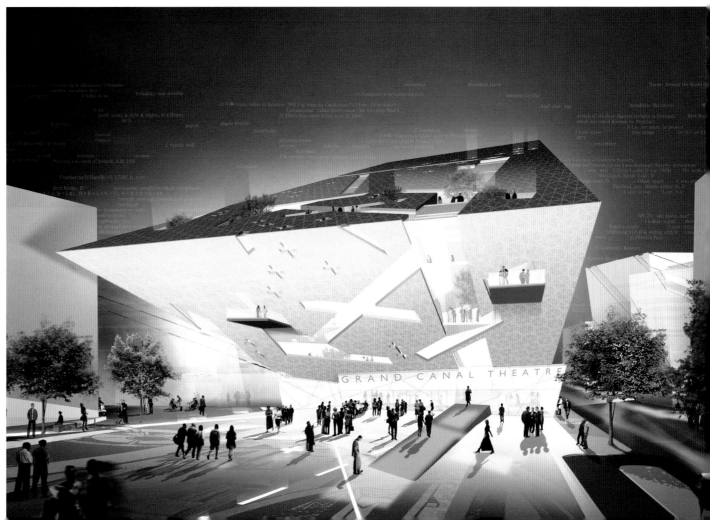

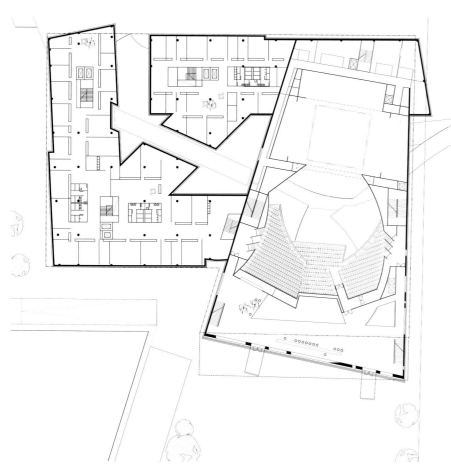

Entrance
Piazza

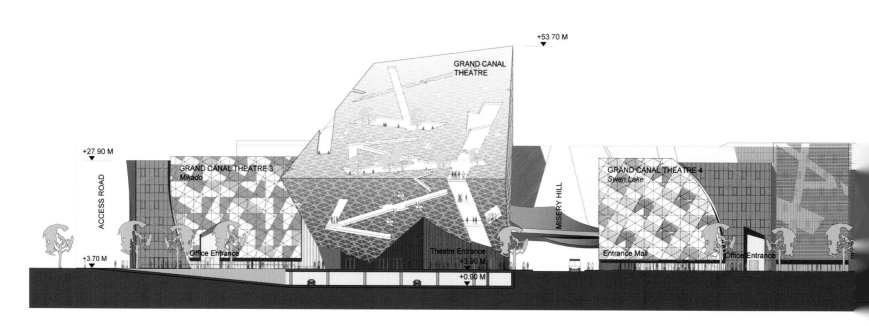

+53.70 M

GRAND CANAL
THEATRE

+27.90 M

GRAND CANAL THEATRE 3
Mikado

GRAND CANAL THEATRE 4
Swan Lake

ACCESS ROAD

MISERY HILL

Office Entrance

Theatre Entrance

Entrance Mall

Office Entrance

+3.70 M

+3.90 M

+0.90 M

Office

Restaurant/
Terrace

Support

Restaurant

Fly Tower

Offices/Support

Garden

Back Stage

Stage

Theatre

Foyer

Bar

Support

Trap

Pit

Terrace

Ticketting

Retail

Lobby

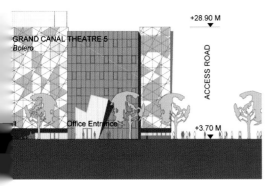

GRAND CANAL THEATRE 5
Bolero

+28.90 M

ACCESS ROAD

Office Entrance

+3.70 M

of the building to its function, instilling real drama into the architecture.

The theatre complex consists of five halls, with the four smaller spaces contained in rectangular structures on each side of the larger main auditorium. This hall is located within the bowels of the imposing rhomboid structure, its form totally hidden on the outside by an outer layer of ancillary spaces between the auditorium and the façade. These ancillary spaces house ticketing and retail services, as well as lobbies squeezed in at the lower levels. Foyers, gardens and bars at the upper levels take advantage of the views over the piazza, and restaurants, terraces and offices are located on top.

Libeskind claims the building is of the twenty-first century in terms of ecological and economic criteria. "The building will

harness the energy of the sun and take advantage of all cutting-edge technologies to ensure that it is a sustainable building. The roof structure of the theatre is designed as a garden overlooking the piazza with spectacular views out over Dublin Bay."

Opposite top and above: Site plan and section. The overhanging foyer allows a far greater floor area than the building's footprint would suggest.

Left: The elevation shows the varied façade treatments. The main volume of the theatre is constructed from glass.

Client
Devey Group
Capacity
2000
Area
40,000 sq. m/430,400 sq. ft
Cost
£85.8m/$158m/€ 125.7m

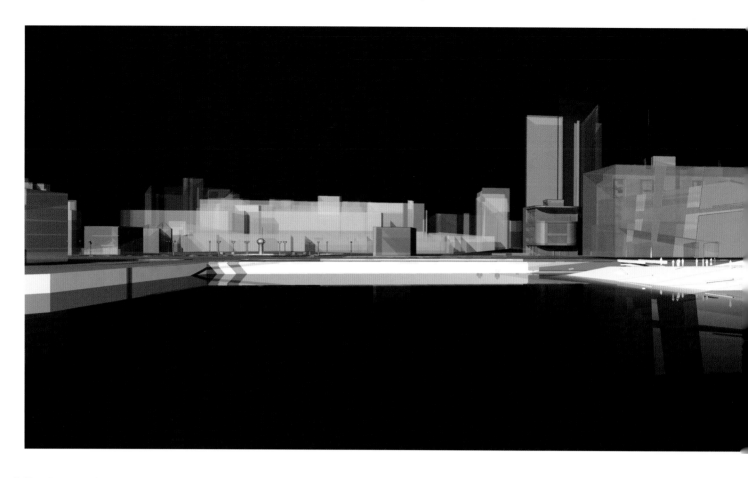

NATIONAL OPERA HOUSE
SNØHETTA
OSLO, NORWAY 2008

A decaying quarter of Oslo has been regenerated by the construction of this new opera house on the site of a disused sawmill at the edge of the Oslo Fjord. The building of a new opera house was the subject of debate for over a hundred years. The Norwegian Opera had had no official home since its foundation in 1957, hence the symbolic importance of the new design. The brief called for something monumental that would provide Norway with a national focus. It seems entirely appropriate that local practice Snøhetta, who were celebrating international acclaim for their newly completed Alexandria Library in Egypt, should win the competition to realize the city's long-awaited dream. Their design for the vast African project shows the level of imagination and the sculptural qualities that were required for Oslo's opera house.

As in the case of many brownfield sites, the legacy of previous industry created major challenges. For more than a century the sawmill had dumped sawdust – contaminated with heavy metals from previous industrial use – into the fjord. As it was gradually covered with layers of silt, its decomposition slowed and the resulting growth of bacteria polluted the water.

Snøhetta's challenge was to contain the environmental impact of the pollutant by disposing carefully of the removed sawdust, as well as to overcome the structural problems associated with building half on land and half in water. The enormous foundation piles have been designed for a life of three hundred years.

Looking beyond conventional opera-house design, the architects explored the concept of 'social monumentality': seeking a powerful architecture that has people at its centre. Part of the outcome was an over-sailing plane that rises from the fjord, creating a concrete beach. From it, people can swim in the water or climb on to the roof for a panoramic view of the city. Craig Dykers of Snøhetta believes that many public buildings are developed around commercial opportunities. Here he was striving for the opposite: to allow people to interact with the building in ways that would not involve them spending money.

The building had to be extremely low to connect both topographically and politically with the city. This decision resolved the architectural challenges but, in turn, created volume and acoustic problems. Visually, the split-level building

is intriguing, and from some angles almost resembles a Stealth bomber; this comparison is not lost on Dykers, who readily pointed out that the cost of the bomber totals $900m (excluding the bombs), whereas that of the opera house is a tiny proportion of this.

The name of the building is, in fact, misleading, because the venue supports the performance of ballet as well as opera. In many respects these two art forms have opposing requirements: opera wants intimacy and a smaller stage, while ballet often needs much more space. Lighting and acoustic demands are also very different. Without the space to create two halls to serve these different performing arts, the architects and acoustic consultants Arup Acoustics had to use their ingenuity to incorporate the required flexibility. The main auditorium is in the shape of a horseshoe and will require no artificial amplification; instead its surfaces are carefully planned to reflect sound around the hall. The smaller hall, rectangular in plan, is for more varied performances than just opera and ballet, and its acoustics are accordingly more flexible. Reverberation in this space can be reduced to accommodate

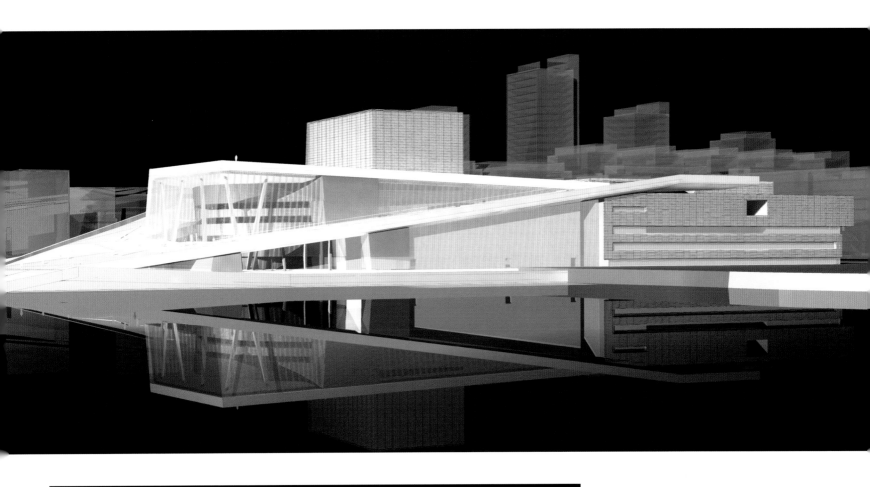

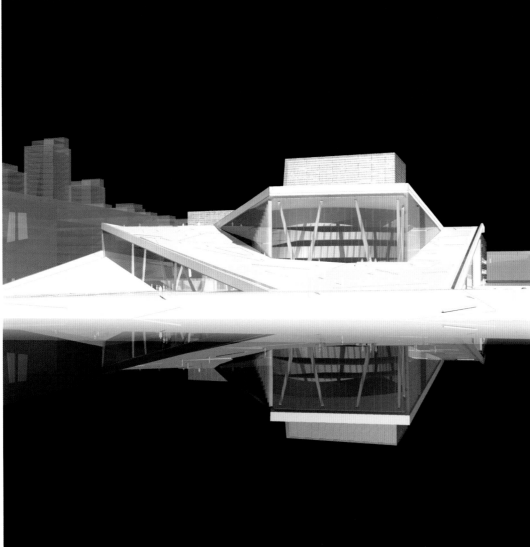

Above: The opera house's public areas slope downwards towards the fjord, creating an unusual focus. The two ramps function partly as the roof of the foyer.

Left: The opera house seen across the water. The wooden drum of the auditorium volume is clearly legible, even from a distance.

Left: Snøhetta's design, with its sleek lines, has been likened to a Stealth bomber.

Bottom: The roof is accessible at various levels, as a viewing terrace and swimming platform.

Opposite, top: Inclined pillars of white marble carry the roof/ramp.

Opposite, centre: The oak-clad volume of the concert hall is a striking part of the foyer, which will contain integrated artwork by Olafur Eliasson.

Opposite, bottom: The auditorium is largely clad in oak. The 'Metafoil' curtain is by the artist Pae White.

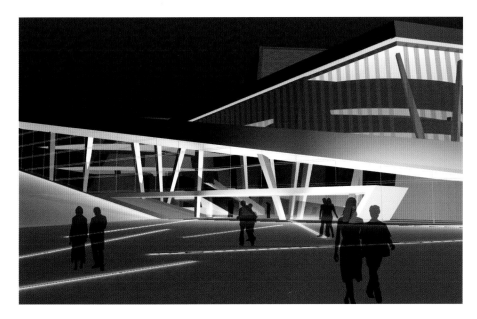

electronically amplified sound, such as that required for musicals and modern opera. There is also a rehearsal studio that is open to the public.

Public opinion about the building was volatile, and the feeling was that such a large sum of money could have been spent on hospitals or schools instead, so Snøhetta had to champion the cultural benefits of the building. Despite having a younger audience in Norway than in many other European countries, opera is still perceived as an 'older' person's interest. The architects were at pains to distinguish their building from venues that they believe had been tainted with this image, such as Glyndebourne in the UK. Instead, they have produced a contemporary structure to which young people can relate. However, politics and financial constraints intervened during the design process, and Dykers admits that they only incorporated half the features originally planned. They retained the 90-m (300-ft) foyer running through the building, and the private garden for back-of-house staff and performers; but the controversial balconies for smoking did not make it off the drawing board. The architects were also under considerable pressure to use Norwegian materials but believed that this was restrictive, arguing that while they saw no reason to avoid local materials, opera itself is not solely Norwegian and involves the constant import and export of ideas. White Italian marble and darker Norwegian granite dominate the exterior, and wood, largely oak, is used extensively inside.

Dykers maintains that there was not a particular architectural inspiration for the National Opera House, but it has been likened to Sydney's Opera House because of its sculptural form. He likes to see it as Sydney without the shells on top: "We were influenced by the location more than anything, and by a deep-rooted understanding of the place."

Client
Statsbygg

Capacity
1350 (main auditorium)
400 (flexible theatre)
200 (rehearsal room)

Area
38,500 sq. m/415,000 sq. ft

Cost
£215m/$400m/€315m

WEST KOWLOON CULTURAL DISTRICT
FOSTER AND PARTNERS

HONG KONG 2008

Above: The vast canopy rises at the eastern end of the site to accommodate a variety of venues.

Opposite, from top: The 'pleasure garden' extends along the waterfront; the main arena will seat thousands and be a venue for all types of performance.

As the world's population steadily increases, towns are growing into cities and cities into conurbations; a humble theatre or even a grand opera house is not sufficient to service the leisure demands of one of these great population centres. The new super-city needs its own dedicated cultural zone or district.

In April 2001, the Hong Kong government launched a competition for such a district on a 40-ha (100-acre) waterfront site at the southern tip of the West Kowloon Reclamation, overlooking Hong Kong Island. This spectacular integrated arts, cultural and entertainment area is intended to "consolidate Hong Kong's reputation as a cultural destination while providing an iconic architectural image for the city", and is part of the plan to make the most of the city's most beautiful asset, Victoria Harbour. The cultural district is described by the government as "Hong Kong's very own 'West End' with a Broadway skyline".

Foster and Partners' design (with associate architects Rocco Design Ltd and acoustic consultants Arup Acoustics) won the commission against fierce competition from Philip Y.K. Liao, Minoru Takeyama, Alan Macdonald/Urbis-LPT and Rocco Yim. Announcing the winner in 2002, Lord Rothschild said, "the signature feature of the design, a great canopy, flows over the various spaces contained within the development to create a unique landmark. The sinuously flowing form of the site contours and the canopy produce a memorable effect." The jury was particularly impressed that even at the conceptual level Foster had organized the site to take full advantage of its prime waterfront location and its proximity to Kowloon Park and the Canton Road retail district.

The design's distinctiveness and coherence will make it immediately recognizable within Hong Kong and an icon around the world; and such an image suits the authorities' desire to create the impression of a modern and progressive Hong Kong. The scheme is largely horizontal, and so does not compete with the tall buildings behind, but rather will become a counterpoint to them. The elements are logically and yet imaginatively arranged, in order to entice people through the commercial and entertainment parts to the cultural centre beyond. There is a balance between public and private interests, and in the mix of arts facilities offered, and the complex is particularly rich in provision of public spaces at various scales. As part of the plan, a substantial park is to be introduced into the heart of Hong Kong, bringing symbolic and practical benefits to this dense urban environment.

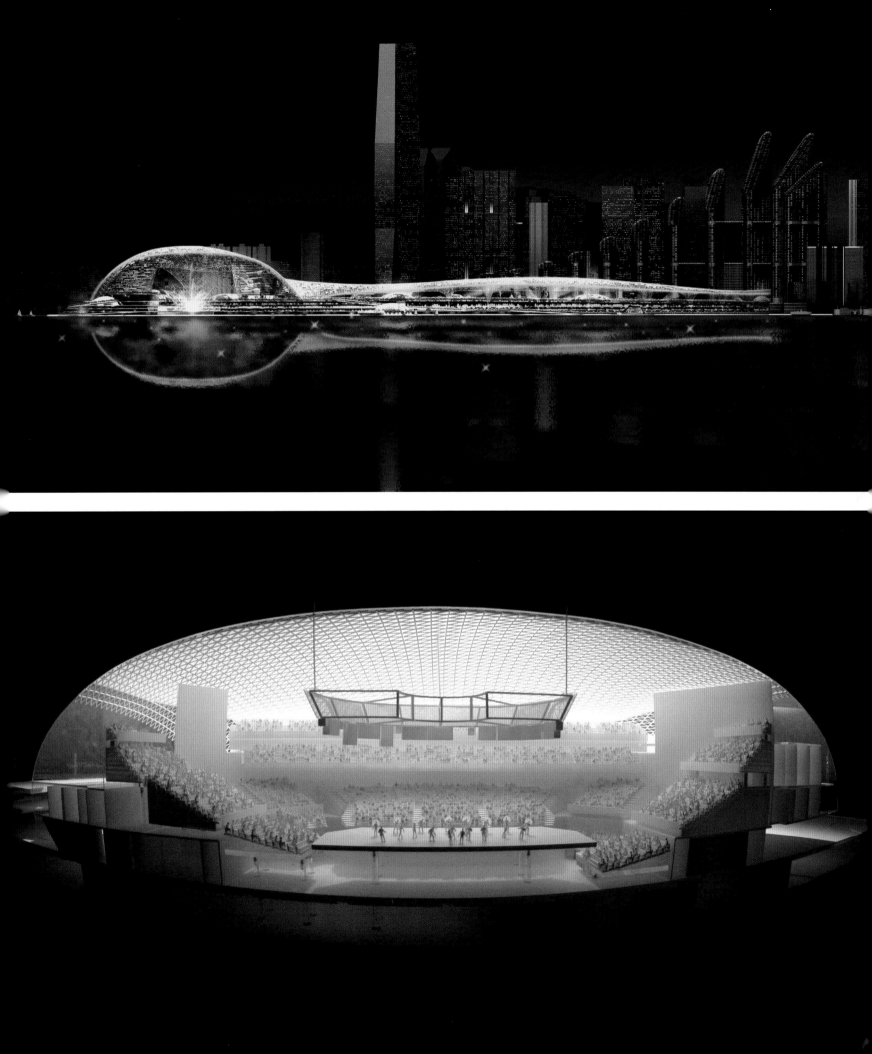

Under the canopy will be a world of entertainment. Public space is a hugely important part of the masterplan, and will include at least four squares. Theatres (opposite), an art gallery and a water amphitheatre (above) will also feature.

Despite its individuality, the new district will be skilfully integrated with the surrounding areas, and in particular will have excellent links to Kowloon Station and Kowloon Park and the associated transit system. As far as the practicalities are concerned, most of the scheme is technically straightforward, and even its large roof is well within current technological capabilities. The lagoon has caused some concern, and is seen as being impractical; although it is likely that a similar public space will be constructed, including a body of water disconnected from the harbour.

Under the eastern end of the canopy will be a mind-boggling array of entertainment venues including a museum of modern art, a major performance space, and an assortment of theatres and concert halls. Over in the west, along the spine and by the harbour will be cinemas, restaurants, shops and other leisure facilities.

Having recently completed Hong Kong's vast new airport at Chek Lap Kok, the practice is well positioned to deliver this complex scheme; and it also brings its vast experience of transportation and movement of people to the project. Hong Kong's *Blade Runner*-style horizontal escalator system will be extended through the park at an elevation of 7 m (23 ft), affording visitors views of Victoria Harbour and the city's famous skyline as they are transported sedately across the park. Such a futuristic system is a fitting part of an architectural and landscaping plan that is intended to reinvent Hong Kong for the twenty-first century.

Client
Dynamic Star International
(Cheung Kong Holdings and Sun Hung Kai Properties)

Capacity
2000, 800, 400 (theatres)
10,000 (main venue)

Area
100,000 sq. m/
1,076,000 sq. ft

Cost
Not available

NEW MARIINSKI THEATRE
DOMINIQUE PERRAULT ARCHITECTE
ST PETERSBURG, RUSSIA 2009

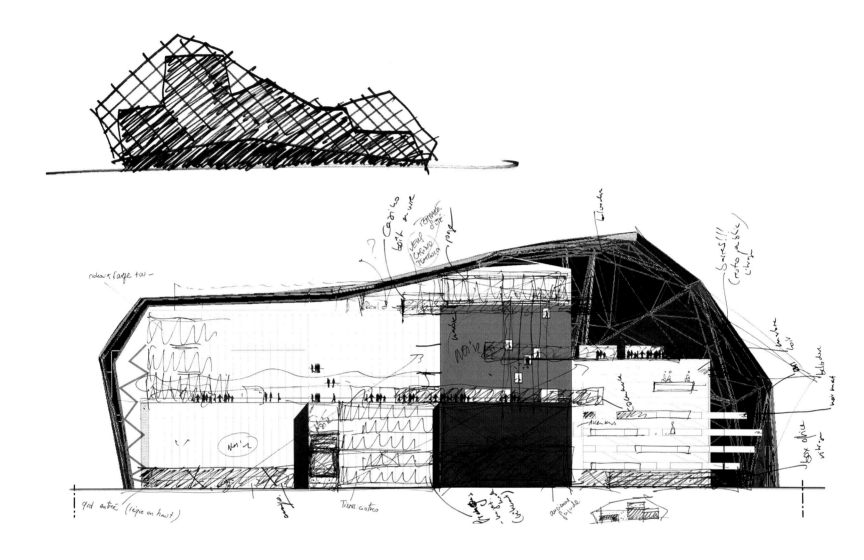

An extraordinarily ambitious performing-arts project, the New Mariinski Theatre sits alongside one of Russia's cultural icons, the classical Mariinski Theatre built in 1860. The integration of such a bold contemporary design within an area rich in architectural heritage is a significant challenge: Perrault cannot afford to deliver simply 'good' architecture; it must be spectacular. What is unique here is that the old will not give way to the new, by being either rebuilt or demolished, but that the two buildings will remain side by side.

Perrault's solution is extraordinarily brave. Realizing that he could not attempt to 're-create' St Petersburg's inherent classicism with any integrity, he has produced one of the most futuristic designs imaginable. "Two projects cohabit to create a single one, unique and inseparable: one focused on setting up the pragmatic and rational tool of the opera, the other weaving links with the surrounding context, allowing the public access to marvel at the heart of the mystery, to penetrate the architecture, rise with it, live the opulence of this art."

The essence of the design is a functional 'box-like' theatre in black marble cocooned within a freestanding glazed structure. Perrault explains: "Visible like St Petersburg's other major monuments, the golden cocoon does not conform to the building's shape. Like a garment of light, it is broadly deployed 'around the body', leaving free spaces, open to the city." The gleaming gold of the cladding responds to the city's many bright cupolas. Construction of the cocoon is complex, with a primary structure of steel trusses and tensioned cables supporting outer and inner secondary systems. The exterior cladding consists of aluminium lamella slats with a gold anodized finish. The glazing is fixed to the inside face leaving a 2-m (6-ft) void for maintenance.

In developing the design, Perrault has taken full advantage of the space between the organic envelope and the rectilinear form it encloses. This space is transformed at the upper levels into terraces, balconies and belvederes, providing views of the city through the enclosing structure. Elsewhere the void incorporates the spectacular foyer, a public restaurant, staff cafés, a summer terrace and other public spaces. The upper levels are accessible day and night during shows, rehearsals, set construction and dismantling. Here, as in Paul Andreu's Oriental Art Centre in Shanghai (pp. 90–93) and Michael Wilford's Esplanade National Performing Arts Centre in Singapore (pp. 65–67), Perrault has recognized the

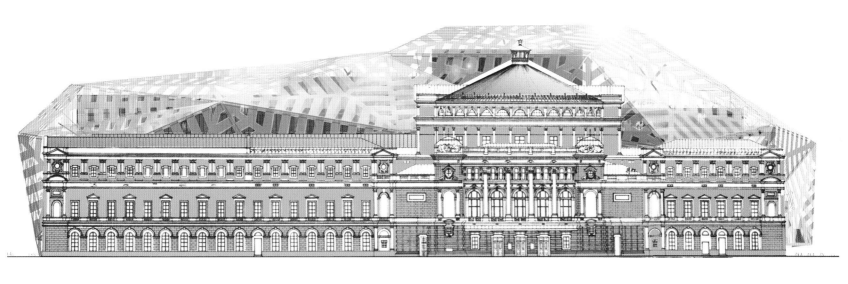

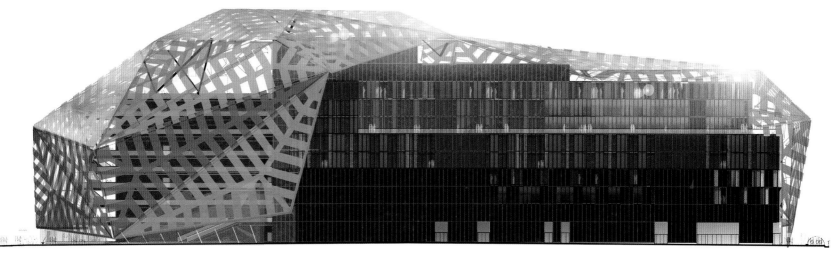

Opposite: The theatre's rectangular form is disguised by being enclosed in an irregular glazed structure.

Above, from top: From the east, the new building peers over the existing Mariinski Theatre; the west and south façades show the black box breaking out of its glass shell.

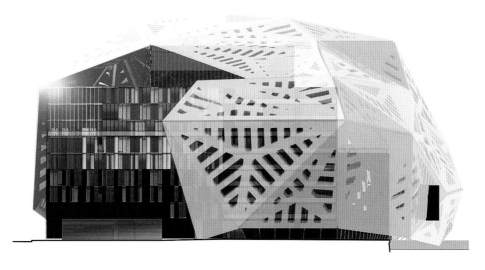

importance of engaging the public, drawing them into the peripheral areas with exciting spaces. The benefits of this are wider acceptance of the project and increased audiences, as casual visitors get intrigued by the workings of the theatre and want to see more.

On the western elevation, adjoining Minsky Lane, the 'black box' theatre breaks out from behind the cocoon and presents an imposing flank of black marble contrasting with the curvaceous form of the main enclosure. On the opposite side, the original Mariinski Theatre frowns across the Krykov Canal at its offspring. Here, Perrault has daringly linked the theatres with a telescopic bridge for transfer of equipment in addition to an underground tunnel for public use.

Inside the theatre box, which is 50 m (160 ft) high, flamboyance disappears and functionality takes over. Vast areas have been given over to the vital support and ancillary functions over its ten levels. Access is via a central spine that crosses the building like an indoor street, connecting all the opera's backstage functions.

Performances in the main auditorium will include ballets, operas and symphonic concerts. Smaller musical events are catered for by the 350-seat chamber-music hall. The interior is decorated in a traditional theme, described by Perrault: "One enters a painting, a tapestry inspired by the ornamentation of our most beautiful classical opera houses. Here we are in a pictorial universe adding a whiff of fantasy to the opera's lyrical dimension."

Top: The new theatre will provide an unusual addition to the canalside streetscape.

Left: The auditorium is sumptuously fitted out in traditional red.

Opposite: The overarching structure lifts from its contact points to allow access to the foyer.

Client
Russian Ministry of Culture

Capacity
2000 (theatre)
350 (chamber-music hall)

Area
65,000 sq. m/700,000 sq. ft

Cost
£150m/$276.6m/€ 220m

METROPOLITAN KANSAS CITY PERFORMING ARTS CENTER
MOSHE SAFDIE AND ASSOCIATES
KANSAS CITY, MISSOURI, USA 2009

"Great architecture is not the goal. Iconic reference is not the goal. Symbolic grandeur is not the goal. The goal of any world-class performing-arts centre today must be the enhancement of the experience for the artist, for the audience and, finally, for the myriad of services necessary before great performances can happen in the modern age: everything from administrative offices to parking spaces." So proclaims the mission statement for this major performing-arts project in Kansas City. The client goes on to set out the vision for the building: "It must ... serve as a home for the opera, ballet and symphony orchestra and provide a catalyst for the revitalization and development of down-town Kansas City, as well as a catalyst to get children educated and participating in the arts". The performance targets specified by the client require the building to be capable of hosting 300–500 entertainment events per year and to accommodate as many as 400,000 people altogether in the first year.

International architectural firm Moshe Safdie with associate architects BNIM Architects embarked on the ambitious project with gusto, producing a design that is exciting but still logical. The architects pulled together a strong team, including Yasuhisa Toyota of Tokyo-based firm Nagata Acoustics, a leading engineer in this field, and Richard Pilbrow of Theatre Projects Consultants, one of the foremost theatre and lighting designers in the world with more than six hundred projects in sixty countries to his credit. Both men had carried out acclaimed work on the Walt Disney Concert Hall (pp. 116–19).

Containing three performance spaces – a ballet/opera house, a concert hall and a small multi-purpose hall – this is a vast building, but then the number of people to be accommodated is also huge. Even from the outside, the visitor will be impressed by three distinct elements: the imposing front elevation with its vast glazed multi-level atrium and curved roof sections defining the different performing spaces; the rear elevation with its appearance of 'stacked cans'; and the breathtaking lobby space with its balconies reminiscent of Frank Lloyd Wright's Guggenheim Museum in New York.

The auditoria are logically placed along the ridgeline of the site. The glazed foyer serves the two major halls, and a smaller foyer is attached to the third space. As the site slopes down to the south, the road cuts under the foyer, forming a generous drop-off area. From here patrons proceed to a lower lobby, which opens to the view south and the terraced gardens, and then enter the main lobby by a grand staircase or elevator.

The client saw the grand lobby as the key element in creating a 'shared experience' inside the building where all visitors mingle and create a buzz of excitement.

Opposite: The rear elevation is highly unusual. The stainless steel cladding anchors the glass of the front façade.

This page: The glazed foyer links the three auditoria, which are clearly differentiated behind it (above) and in plan (left). A terrace slopes away from the building, which sits on a ridge.

The enveloping structure of the complex is a series of undulating, vertical segments of a circle forming the northern container of the backstage areas. As these elements ascend, they create a segmented, gently curving crown to the building. From this crest, the roof descends in a curve following the toroidal geometry of light cables and stainless steel. The roof intersects with an outwardly inclined and curved glass wall, which contains the south-facing foyer. The tensile forces of the suspended glass foyer roof are counteracted by a series of cables anchoring the structure at the entrance terrace. The curved, segmented northern walls are sheathed in stainless steel and punctuated by acid-etched, limestone-coloured, pre-cast concrete perpendicular walls. The theatre façades are clad in beech panels forming continuous curved, stacked balconies. The various lounges form sculptural shapes visible under the glass structure. This transparency opens the foyer to striking views of the skyline, and at night the dramatically lit theatre façades and the activity in the public areas can be seen from outside, allowing the "glow of sophisticated urbanity" to entice people from afar.

Below: Studies of the roof show the segmented back wall and the anchoring of the tensile structure to the front (top) and the arrangement of the interior spaces (bottom).

Opposite top: Atmospheric lighting defines the vertical segments containing the backstage areas.

Opposite bottom: The public concourse linking the three auditoria is roofed with glass held up by cables.

Client
The Metropolitan Kansas
City Performing Arts
Center, Inc.
Capacity
1800 (ballet theatre)
1600 (concert hall)
250 (multi-use hall)
Area
18,000 sq. m/200,000 sq. ft
Cost
£177m/$326m/€260m

203

Together with the Dee and Charles Wyly Theater (pp. 206–9), this building falls within a masterplan created by Foster and Partners for the development of the Dallas Center for the Performing Arts. The ambitious plan is being realized by a quartet of winners of the Pritzker Prize, the world's highest award for architecture – Rem Koolhaas (of OMA), I.M. Pei, Renzo Piano and Lord Foster – and is therefore guaranteed to put Dallas on the cultural map. The new buildings are set along a 'green spine' formed by Flora Street, a pedestrian-friendly environment designed to be accessible and legible, with plazas, gardens and a canopy of trees linking the Foster and Koolhaas buildings.

Facing the Grand Plaza and the Annette Strauss Artist Square performing space, the Margot and Bill Winspear Opera House will provide a focal point for the whole district. Foster, working with associate architects Kendall/Heaton, aims to question the fundamentals of opera-going: "What is the nature of the opera house in the twenty-first century; and how can we create a building that offers a model for the future?" His answer is to reinvent the conventional typology of the opera house, opening out its closed, hierarchical form to create a transparent and welcoming series of spaces that wrap around the rich red-stained drum of the 2000-seat auditorium. His ambition was to "create a building that not only fully integrated with the cultural life of Dallas, but which would become a destination in its own right for the non-opera-going public, with a restaurant, café and bookstore that will be publicly accessible throughout the day".

The recognition of the need to break down the barriers – both physical and psychological – surrounding opera forms a key theme throughout this book. It must be the single most important problem facing the performing-arts industry – the development of a 'sustainable' audience for the new century.

Foster's design makes a bold visual statement with its dominant canopy stretching out into the square – a physical blurring of the boundaries to follow through the ideology. Reaching out to passers-by and opera-goers alike, it provides a communal space that is not only part of the complex but also in the public domain.

DALLAS CENTER FOR THE PERFORMING ARTS
MARGOT AND BILL WINSPEAR OPERA HOUSE
FOSTER AND PARTNERS
DALLAS, USA 2009

Client
Dallas Center for the Performing Arts Foundation
Capacity
2000
Area
18,400 sq. m/198,000 sq. ft
Cost
Not available

Above left: The slatted canopy will provide a shaded environment for outside events.

Above: At the heart of the complex is the theatre with its many balconies. A traditional horseshoe shape was chosen for acoustic quality.

Below: Cutaway drawing, showing the transition from outside spaces into the auditorium, via the plaza and the glazed atrium.

Left: The red drum of the auditorium is surrounded by transparent public space, independent of the opera-going experience.

With this theatre, also part of the Foster masterplan for the Dallas Center for the Performing Arts, Rem Koolhaas and his team at OMA have produced a masterful and refreshing design. With such a small footprint, the building is all about verticality. Reaching eleven storeys, with one further level below ground, its rectilinear box form is translucent, allowing views of the intestine-shaped workings inside. A total break visually from OMA's Casa da Musica in Porto, Portugal (pp. 124–27), this design project is brimming with originality.

Koolhaas has used some heavyweight structural engineering to set the building on two massive lever-arms to form a highly unusual space free of columns between the ground and the fourth floor. The transparency afforded by this configuration allows views across this interior plaza through to the other side of the building.

On a more practical level, the theatre's ancillary services are located above and below the auditorium. Offices, rehearsal studios, the costume shop and other support spaces are located in the upper floors, with foyers below and car parking underground. This provides unprecedented flexibility for theatre companies, allowing many different configurations including proscenium, thrust and flat-floor. The stage can be reconfigured in a matter of hours by means of lifts, pulleys, turntables and other mechanical devices. The walls of the Wyly Theater can even be raised to allow the cityscape beyond the park to become part of the scenery of the performance.

The area earmarked for Foster's masterplan is in need of regeneration, and OMA's striking, stacked theatre will play an important part.

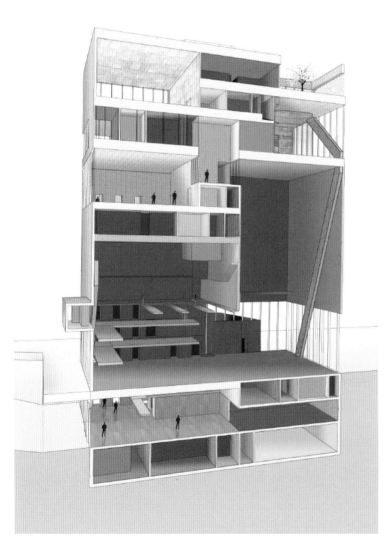

Above: The Wyly Theater is a mysterious addition to the drab urban skyline.

Left and far left: OMA has created spaces of varying heights, to accommodate both intimate social spaces and airy studios.

Bottom: The walls can be removed to allow the cityscape to play a part in the performance.

Opposite top: The remarkable structure appears quite different from each side. Enormous pillars carry the weight and create a plaza underneath.

Opposite, bottom right: The ground floor is transparent and even the walls of the upper storeys can be removed.

Opposite, bottom left: The traditional theatre plan is turned on its head, with all spaces sitting on top of each other.

Client
Dallas Center for the Performing Arts Foundation
Capacity
600
Area
7000 sq. m/75,000 sq. ft
Cost
Not available

ELBE PHILHARMONIC HALL
HERZOG & DE MEURON
HAMBURG, GERMANY 1966/2009

Above: The foyer consists
almost entirely of
stairs. Underneath the
auditorium, it allows
access both to the hall
itself and to observation
galleries looking out
over the harbour.

Opposite: The
amphitheatre-style
concert hall echoes the
structure of the foyer. Its
many balconies ensure
that each member of the
audience has an excellent
line of sight.

Pages 212–13: HDM's
addition appears to float
on top of the warehouse.
The grid of the older
building is continued
in the arrangment of
the apartments and
other spaces in the
new structure.

Fuelled by their spectacular successes in London – the conversion of the derelict Bankside Power Station into Tate Modern and the construction of the award-winning Laban Centre in Deptford – Herzog & de Meuron (HDM) have in this project fused their skills in regeneration and performing spaces to produce a breathtaking structure.

In a similar way to Renzo Piano's Niccolò Paganini Auditorium in Parma (pp. 38–41), which saw the conversion of a sugar factory into a fantastic performance space, this project will transform a derelict cocoa-bean warehouse (the *Kaispecher*) into the centrepiece of Hamburg's cultural life. Surprisingly, these giant industrial buildings of the nineteenth and twentieth centuries are turning out to be models of sustainability, an overworked term often used to justify flimsy modern developments with a design life of a few decades. Here, however, is a structure that can be reused and adapted decades after it was built.

So well built was the original structure that the Elbphilharmonie project will only require minor reinforcement of the warehouse's foundations. HDM's interest was not only structural, however. The ware-house also served visually and architecturally as a base for their design of the new Philharmonic hall: "Shaped like a distorted cube that tapers towards the west, it is at its most elegant at the tip ..., where it shows the greatest urban relevance."

Harbour warehouses such as this intentionally echo the vocabulary of the historical streetscapes, and their brickwork,

fenestration and gables are in keeping with the urban architecture of the time, albeit with significantly greater massing and without windows. The architects made use of one difference apparent in this warehouse: "Although its brickwork conformed contextually to that of its neighbours, its façades displayed an exceptional radicalism and abstraction. The warehouse resembles the clay edifices of the Arabic world with their formwork apertures. Its regular grid of holes measuring 50 x 70 cm (20 x 27½ in.) can hardly be called windows; they serve more as structure than as openings to the world outside."

The modern addition is an extrusion of the warehouse with an identical footprint, in the architects' words "an iridescent multifaceted crystal placed flush on top of the brick Kaispecher". The wide, undulating roof rises to a maximum height of 100 m (328 ft) at the top of the peninsula, and slopes down towards the eastern end, where most of the roof is 20 m (66 ft) lower.

The main entrance is at the east. Like a stairway to heaven, a breathtakingly long escalator will feed visitors up from the quay diagonally across the whole warehouse to the plaza. Sandwiched between the top of the old building and the bottom of the new, this public area will allow light to burst out of the structure at night. It will take advantage of a spectacular panorama of downtown Hamburg to the north and the River Elbe and its sprawling harbour to the east, west and south. In certain places

this terrace will widen into larger outdoor areas whose size, lowered floors and cupola-shaped cut-outs will further heighten the drama of the view. Ancillary areas such as restaurants, bars and the hotel lobby are accessed from here.

The lobby is an 'echo' of or 'overture' to the main concert hall. Located under the auditorium, with the hall's stepped floor as its ceiling, it exists as a dramatic landscape of stairs spilling out in all directions. "Everything is stairs. Floors, ceilings and walls become almost indistinguishable." The main auditorium is reminiscent of a large sweeping amphitheatre with the orchestra and conductor placed in the midst of the audience, and the galleries sweeping into each other.

The Elbe Philharmonic Hall is a much more ambitious project than Tate Modern. As well as the 2200-seat concert hall and 550-seat chamber hall, the complex will house a 220-room hotel, restaurants, a gym, a conference centre and thirty-five apartments. According to the architects, the bold structure "will inject the surrounding neighbourhood with energy and dynamism. Similar cultural 'implants' in other cities provide impressive proof of the way in which such projects contribute substantially to urban renewal, enhancing the attraction of urban districts and, indeed, functioning as agents of change."

Client
Freie Hansestadt
Hamburg
Capacity
2200 (concert hall)
550 (chamber hall)
Area
65,000 sq. m/700,000 sq. ft
Cost
Not available

GUANGZHOU OPERA HOUSE
ZAHA HADID
GUANGZHOU, CHINA 2010

The eyes of the world are on this project: this is the opera house that got away, popping up in the southern reaches of China after the debacle that was the competition to design an opera house for Cardiff. In 1994, Hadid, who was already highly acclaimed but whose work remained largely unbuilt, won the Cardiff competition with a typically bold design, but after much hand-wringing and acrimony the committee lost confidence and handed the project to local architect Percy Thomas (pp. 112–15). It was a cruel blow, as this was Hadid's first big win, but she looked outside her home country (she is British although she was born in Baghdad) to find fame. She is now recognized as one of the most prolific female architects on the planet. Only after gaining this international

recognition did she win her first UK commission, to build the Architecture Foundation's new centre in London.

It is now time for Hadid to show the world what Cardiff missed. Although she is currently engaged in building a string of major projects around the world, she will be aware of the international interest in Guangzhou and has delivered a spectacular design. It should go without saying that this is not a vision transported from Cardiff, but a whole new experience organically grown out of the exciting site next to the Pearl River.

The concept is explained by Hadid: "The Guangzhou Opera House with its tantalizing contours will resonate with the high notes of Chinese opera, in harmony with the tenor of its Western brother. It will

stand alongside its global family as a testament to state-of-the-art architecture, and as a lasting monument to the new millennium. Its unique twin boulder design will enhance urban function with open access to the riverside and dock areas, and at the same time will create a new dialogue with the emerging new town. It is from here that we hope to see the story of Guangzhou continue its evolutionary journey."

The building is an adjunct to the Haixinsha Tourist Park and will eventually form a complex with a museum. When seen from the park at the centre of the Zhujiang Boulevard, the opera house creates a visual prelude to the tourist park beyond. Like many of Hadid's buildings, it does not have a simple form, but rather an amorphous shape that changes depending on the

Right: The sculptural envelope encloses regularly shaped spaces.

Opposite top: The complex provides links to the river and is surrounded by attractive and welcome public space in the built-up city.

Opposite bottom: The foyer glows enticingly through the daring angled façade.

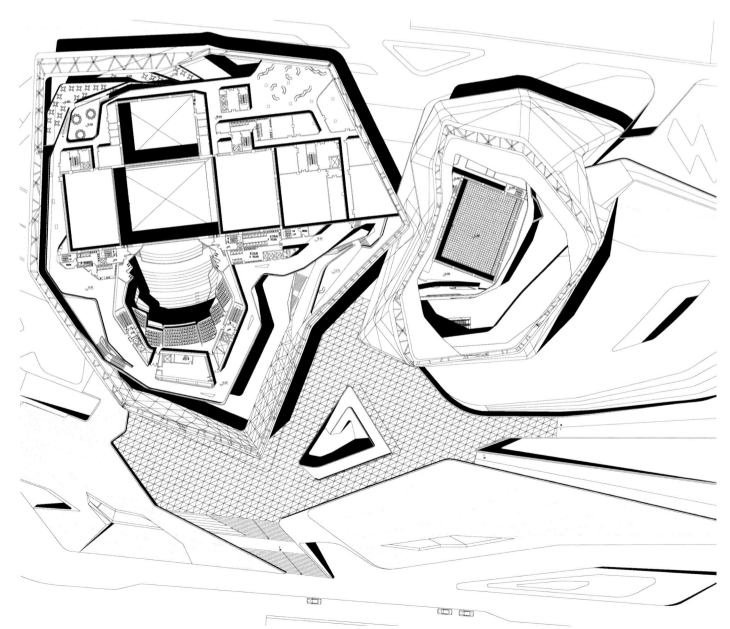

Opposite top: The triangular grid extends above the entrance, where it is supported on slender pillars.

Opposite bottom: In the foyer the triangular grid is seen from inside. The structure is monumental and impressive.

Above: The organic forms of the auditorium produce the effect of a 'moulded' interior.

Pages 218–19: Hadid's low, sinuous structure is part of a wider plan for the development of the area, to include Wilkinson Eyre's proposed twin towers, seen behind.

direction from which it is viewed. The approach offers the most dramatic view, with the vast steps rising towards the building's imposing glazed elevation backed by the spectacular skyscraper skyline of the new town of Zhujiang, including Wilkinson Eyre's twin towers.

Inside, the building shows echoes of Hadid's recent work in Germany, the BMW Central Building in Munich and the Science Centre in Wolfsburg. As in many of the projects featured in this book, some of the most exciting spaces are the public areas or transit routes. Hadid's design is an uncompromising celebration of the sculptural form. This is apparent by her original approach to fundamental building elements, such as the glazed elevations that have none of the expected vertical or horizontal support members. Here she has

adopted a matrix of triangles as the structure. This doubles as the glazing supports, producing an impressive fenestration. The glass façade leans outwards as it rises, enhancing the feeling of space inside.

In the main auditorium Hadid surprises again with a Gaudí-like approach to the balconies and walls. The free-flowing organic curves and shapes set the building apart from the two other opera houses being completed in China, in Shanghai and Beijing (both by Parisian architect Paul Andreu; pp. 90–93 and 180–83), which, while being clearly contemporary and in many ways radical, pay much more homage to tradition.

Client
City of Guangzhou
Capacity
1800
Area
70,000 sq. m/753,500 sq. ft
Cost
£65m/$120m/€95.4m

LYRIC THEATRE
O'DONNELL + TUOMEY
BELFAST, UK

The commission for the new Lyric Theatre, on the site of the current building, was won in an open international competition in 2003 by O'Donnell + Tuomey, a Dublin-based practice founded in 1988 by Sheila O'Donnell and John Tuomey, both formerly of James Stirling Michael Wilford and Associates in London. Construction of the theatre has not yet begun, but plans for funding are currently in progress.

The project's prominent location on a triangular plot beside Belfast's Lagan River plays a large part in the proposal. The architects explain the principles of the design: "The Lyric stands amongst trees on sloping ground beside the Lagan. Seen from the river, it is an object building in parkland, a luminous, translucent presence. On Ridgeway Street, the Lyric holds one corner of a continuous system of brick streets, the last building in the grid. The Lyric belongs to the street and to the river. It is anchored to its site, built in angular Belfast brick, and it is floating in the Lagan haze, with flowing spaces for public circulation. It is embedded, permanent, here to stay and dynamic, fluid, open to change."

Externally the theatre is expressed as a brick and crystalline form. The foyer is approached up a gentle ramp from the street, and makes full use of the building's setting with a long bar overlooking the Lagan. A stairway leads to the upper foyer, which overlooks the street and provides access to both theatres, the green room and the terrace. The lift, toilets and cloakrooms are all contained within the theatre's brick walls.

The seating in the 400-seat main auditorium is configured in an uninterrupted single steep rake, with the furthest seat an intimate 17 rows, 15.5 m (34.5 ft), from the stage. The hall is timber-lined for acoustic purposes. A forestage 3 m (9 ft) deep can be added by removing the first three rows of seats. The second auditorium, a smaller studio space, has galleries on three sides to allow courtyard staging, as well as flexible seating for traverse, end-stage and in-the-round performances.

Above and opposite bottom: The solid brick auditorium is enclosed by a layer of public spaces constructed primarily from glass.

Opposite top: The entrance foyer is highly transparent, allowing the building to interact with its surroundings.

The theatre's reinforced-concrete structural frame is designed to stabilize the building and support its long spans and cantilevers, and the theatre and studio are structurally independent to ensure acoustic integrity. Climate-control systems are integrated into the structure – air plenums in the support for the raked seating and extract ducts concealed in voids in the external walls – and natural ventilation is employed where possible to ensure the energy efficiency of the building. The foyers and circulation areas are kept at a broadly constant temperature by the thermal mass of exposed concrete slabs. Stairs, corridors and stage facilities are all fully accessible, and all levels are connected by lifts.

The architects have clearly taken pains to make the experience of the building exciting and enjoyable for performers, staff and public alike. They have provided visitors with glimpses of the centre's private activities: making them aware of what is going on in the translucent rehearsal room floating above the entrance, for example, but maintaining the performers' privacy by showing movement only, in the form of shapes and shadows. River views are provided for performers and staff from this room and also from the wing with laundry/wardrobe/dressing areas, which has small round windows in a witty allusion to the washing machines that are so important to the theatre's backstage life.

Cantilevers are a dominant part of the structural design – even the administration wing is located on a mezzanine over the box office overlooking the foyer. O'Donnell + Tuomey have used the topography to good effect and indeed the entire concept has been driven by it. The sloping site enables the provision of parking for twenty cars along a one-way ramped route underneath the circulation system above. Truck delivery to the backstage scenery dock is off the street and undercover, below the theatre itself; front of house, the café opens on to a landscaped terrace with walkways leading to Stranmillis Embankment. As a piece of design with its own logic but also integrated with its setting, the Lyric Theatre cannot be faulted, and once funding is secured Belfast will have a valuable addition to its cultural life.

Below and opposite bottom: The brick form of the auditorium rises from the lower, more regular foyer and circulation spaces.

Bottom: The design uses the more awkward parts of the triangular site to increase the green space around the theatre, creating a visual link to the river.

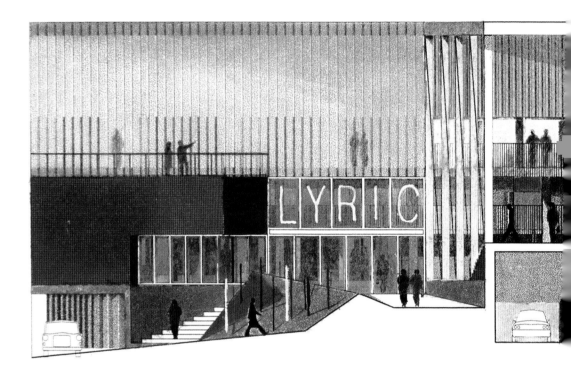

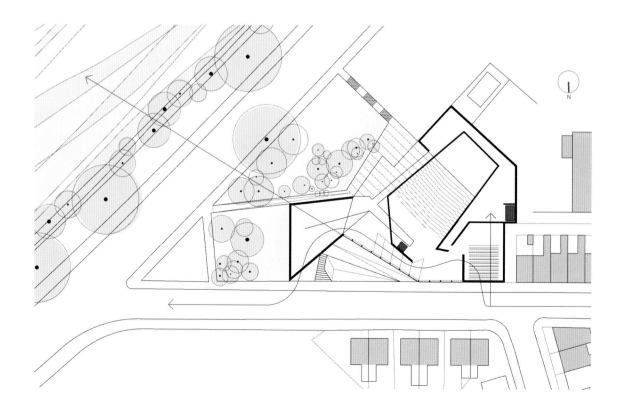

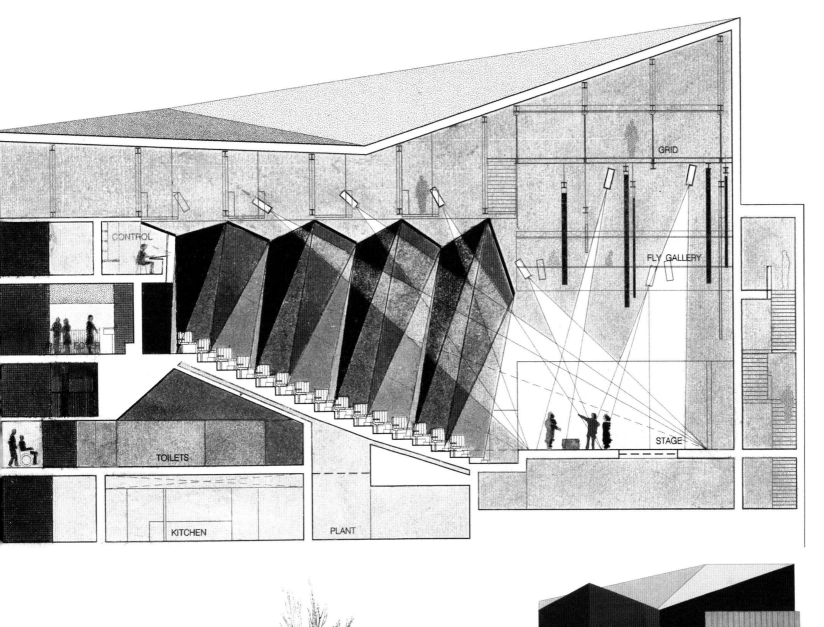

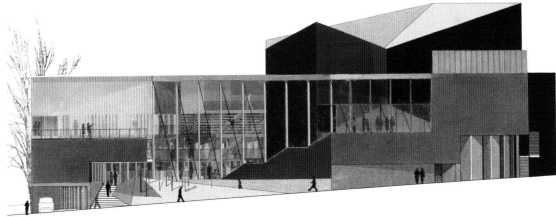

Client
Lyric Theatre, Belfast
Capacity
400 (theatre); 150 (studio)
Area
4,300 sq. m/46,000 sq. ft
Cost
Not available

NEW GLOBE THEATER
FOSTER AND PARTNERS
NEW YORK, USA

Castle Williams, located on the north-west corner of Governor's Island (just south of Manhattan), was built in 1811 and is considered to be one of the finest examples of coastal fortification in the United States. Occupied by the military for nearly two centuries, it was opened to the public in 1996, and a brave plan directed by Barbara Romer, founder of the New Globe Theater (a not-for-profit organization dedicated to this project), has recently emerged to bring the castle fully back into the public realm by converting it into a world-class performance venue.

Foster and Partners has been working closely with the owners, the US National Park Service (NPS), on a proposal to replicate the form of London's Globe Theatre within the walls of the castle. The decaying structure is to be brought to life by a formidable team of experts including theatre consultants Battle McCarthy and Arup Acoustics.

The NPS brief is challenging and includes strict guidelines. Castle Williams's historic structure must be preserved and its deterioration halted. The history of the area must be presented in an exhibition space and the majestic views out from the castle retained. There must be access to all areas, independent of theatrical operations. The new building must be an intimate performance space with the flexibility to accommodate different types of productions, a cultural icon with international appeal that will give Castle Williams added visibility in New York Harbour. Lastly, consistent with the great concern for the area's heritage, the works must be completely reversible, so that the new additions can be removed in the future without damaging the monument.

To work within the bounds of such a seemingly restrictive brief would appear at first to eliminate any prospect of exciting architecture. This is all part of the challenge for the design team, however, and an exciting scheme has bubbled up through the cracks in the brief. The architects have worked closely with preservationists on the new design, which includes a new roof canopy protecting the courtyard elevation of the castle. Visitors enter the building through the castle's heavy stone defences and pass into a fully glazed five-storey foyer. Internal circulation is contained in a top-lit 'transition zone' separating the old castle and the new auditorium. The castle

structure can be seen through the glass enclosure of the auditorium. An audience capacity of 1200 will be split between 800 in the gallery and 400 standing. A new roof-level bar will boast outstanding views stretching from the Verrazano Bridge to the Brooklyn Bridge and taking in the Statue of Liberty, Ellis Island and Manhattan.

The new theatre will be positively brimming with new technology. Firstly, Arup Acoustics' Soundlab system has been used to capture the acoustic fingerprint of the original Globe Theatre, through its replica on London's South Bank. This is used to generate a digital model, which then helps define an acoustic brief to determine the configuration of the auditorium and its finishes. The result should be a performing space with identical acoustic characteristics to London's Globe.

In line with the Leadership in Energy and Environmental Design certification requirements, Battle McCarthy has developed a comprehensive low-energy, passive design solution to minimize environmental impact with the aid of detailed analysis. The thermal mass of the castle is used as a 'heat sink' to minimize the energy required to heat or cool the auditorium, and a sun-tracking shade, calibrated to the sun's annual path, prevents the glazed transition zone from overheating.

But what does the management of London's Globe think about this new twin across the pond? Peter Kyle, the Executive Director of Shakespeare's Globe in London, said, "Assiduous research, meticulous planning, boundless enthusiasm and an unswervable devotion to a lofty ideal. These are the qualities that built Shakespeare's Globe, here in London, and it is because I see these same qualities in Barbara Romer's vision for a New Globe in New York that we are partnering with her to help realize this world-class dream."

Above: The approach to the theatre's entrance. The glazed space between the original walls and the new auditorium contains stairs to the theatre balconies.

Left: The theatre is set out in the same way as the early-seventeenth-century building on which it is modelled, with 'groundlings' standing in the centre to watch the performance. Its sophisticated technology, however, belongs firmly in the twenty-first century.

Opposite: The predominantly glass intervention is slotted into the shell of the fort. The canopy over the glazed 'transition zone' moves with the sun to avoid the public areas overheating.

Client
New Globe Theater
Capacity
1200
Area
290 sq. m/3150 sq. ft
Cost
Not available

NATIONAL THEATRE OF CYPRUS
KOHN PEDERSON FOX
NICOSIA, CYPRUS

Kohn Pederson Fox's (KPF) temporary diversion from its ambitious programme of tall buildings to create a small theatre for the Mediterranean island of Cyprus has naturally increased anticipation for this otherwise low-key project. The practice is known worldwide for consistent delivery of high-quality skyscrapers in major metropolises including New York, Hong Kong, Shanghai and London, and its participation in this project must have provoked some interesting discussions among the judging panel of the competition in 2003. However, one does not have to look too far to find the reason for such interest – only one block to the south, KPF's design for the island's House of Representatives is due to be completed simultaneously with the theatre.

The theatre has as its backdrop a public park, a setting that essentially removed any issues of urban context, although it did generate instead the expectation of a 'grand elevation' facing the park. In homage to the island's rich heritage of Roman amphitheatres, the park itself is the location for many outdoor concerts. According to the architects, "the theatre is conceived as a public institution engaged with the community it serves. The design integrates the theatre and public park."

A raised, landscaped berm protects the theatre site, and two ramps lead visitors up from the park into the building, the design of which is a collection of geometric forms with echoes of Michael Wilford's Lowry Performing and Visual Arts Centre in Salford, UK (pp. 32–35). In plan, though, it appears rather like a giant nutcracker, with the main auditorium playing the part of the 'nut'. (One must assume that theatre-goers will not be aware that they are entering such a machine.) Despite its outward simplicity, the theatre is compact and delivers some rewarding spaces. A multi-level foyer flanking the park provides a successful transition between the public space and the theatre experience beyond, as well as views over the park from attractive atrium-like spaces. This rectangular foyer block links the two auditoria – the 550-seat lyric theatre and the 150-seat new theatre – and the leftover space at the heart of the site is used as a garden and courtyard, away from traffic noise, providing light and ventilation to the back of the foyer.

Being organic in form, the main auditorium is easily distinguished from

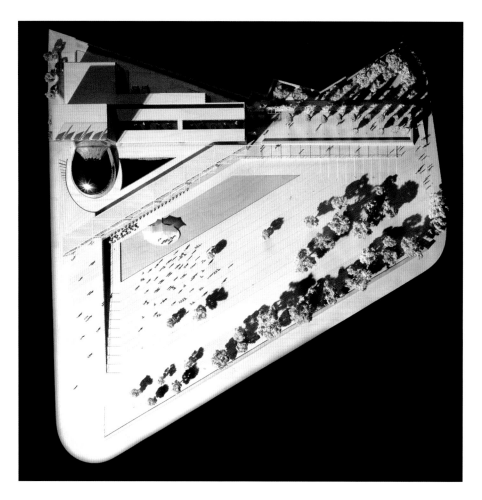

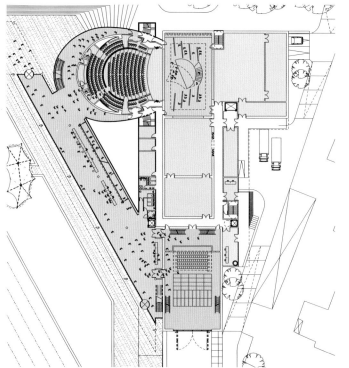

Above: The model in plan view. The lyric theatre is in the blue volume at top left, with the smaller theatre to the right. A large part of the site is taken up by a private terraced garden.

Left: Ground-floor plan. The back-of-house areas are in green, at the north end of the site, and the pink, public areas to the south face the garden and the park. A water garden in the centre brings light and ventilation into the backstage areas.

Opposite: Axonometric of the lyric theatre. The room is designed in three layers: the curve of the gallery fronts, the outside wall of the auditorium, and an outer shell containing lobbies, control rooms and storage areas.

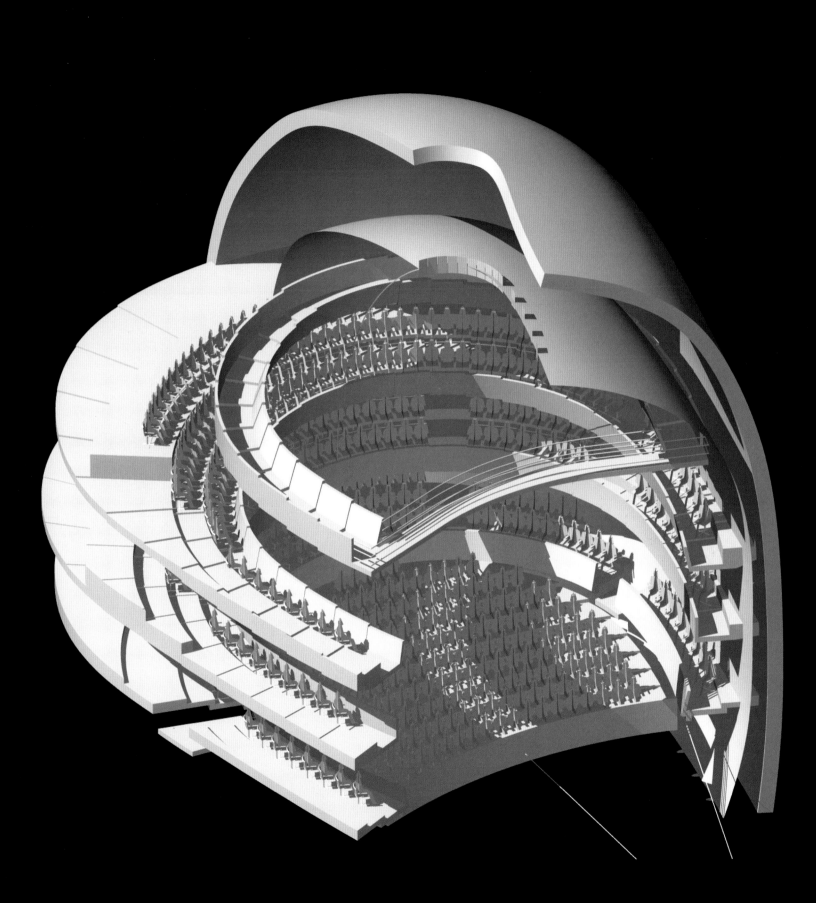

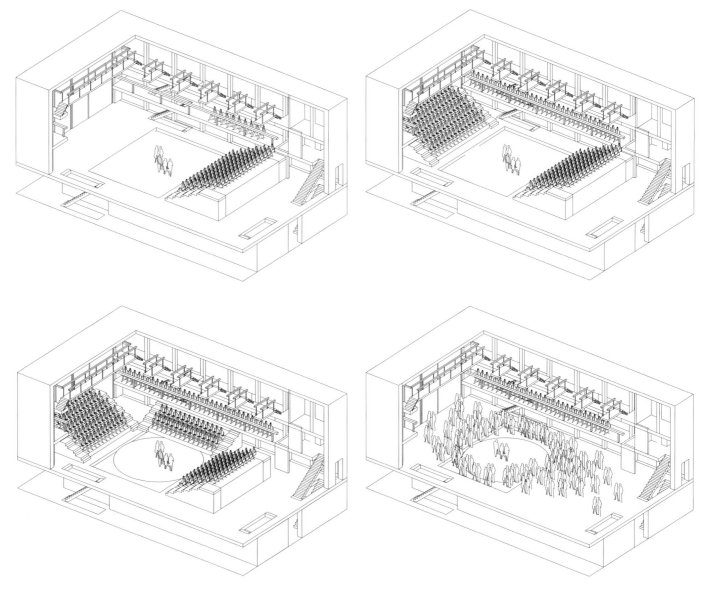

Opposite top: The public foyer overlooks the terrace and the park beyond. Ramps seen within the foyer link the upper levels of the two auditoria.

Opposite bottom: View from the upper circle. The curve of the balconies draws the audience in and engages it fully with the action on the stage.

Right: The smaller theatre is a flexible space that can be used in a variety of ways. The stage can be set at either end (top left), in the centre (top right), or to one side (bottom left). Promenade performances can extend into the garden (bottom right).

the ancillary elements of the theatre and becomes the natural focus of the complex. Glimpses are also allowed from the park through the glazed south elevation of the foyer block. The auditorium is constructed from concrete cast in-situ, with a sequence of ribs of variable geometry that establish the shape of the hall. Fred Pilbrow, director of KPF, explains: "Externally the auditorium volume is the focus of the composition; however, once inside the audience enfolds the stage to create an intimate theatrical environment", the classic 'horseshoe' configuration minimizing the distance from actor to audience. The smaller theatre is conceived as an open-ended workshop space with simple galleries around the perimeter. The design affords a high degree of flexibility: the stage can be set in the centre of the space, at either end, or to one

side of the room, and the auditorium can also accommodate promenade performances that can extend into the private garden beyond.

Administration offices are set at high level, grouped around a courtyard, and enjoy direct connections both to front of house and to backstage areas. This area also contains studio apartments for visiting actors and theatre personnel, overlooking the garden.

As would be expected from international giants KPF, this project solves all the usual problems of circulation, technical performance and all-important public space. But more than that, it will set a benchmark in a city blessed with a vast array of ancient cultural heritage but little high-quality contemporary architecture.

Client
Cyprus Theatre Organization

Capacity
550 (lyric theatre)
150 (new theatre)

Area
5,800 sq. m/62,400 sq. ft

Cost
Not available

MUSIC BOX
FOREIGN OFFICE ARCHITECTS
LONDON, UK

In November 2003, Foreign Office Architects (FOA) won the commission to build the BBC's new £22m music centre in White City, West London. Fighting off stiff competition from leading practices including Future Systems, Zaha Hadid and Ushida Findlay, their bid was no doubt strengthened by their recent success with the Torrevieja Municipal Theatre in Spain (pp. 156–59). Foreign Office Architects is one of Europe's most innovative practices and went on to win the competition for the prestigious stadium for the 2012 Olympic Games in London.

The brownfield site is steeped in history. The name 'White City' derives from the white marble cladding of the buildings put up when it was developed in 1908 for the Franco–English Exhibition. The site was used for the Olympic Games in that same year, and for the Japan–British Exhibition in 1910. It then became a venue for dog racing and athletics until the mid-1980s, when it was acquired and developed by the BBC.

The music centre will form part of the new Media Village, a complex of six buildings masterplanned by London-based architects Allies and Morrison, and will house the BBC Symphony Orchestra, the BBC Symphony Chorus, the BBC Concert Orchestra and the BBC Singers. However, in commissioning the building, the BBC also had another agenda. The organization's primary source of funding, the UK's television licence fee, was coming under increasing criticism and pressure, and so the BBC felt it needed to be more accountable to the licence payer – in short,

it had to show the public where its money was going.

This factor had naturally already started to shape the brief. The BBC's estate consists of some five hundred buildings that are not known for their architectural merit; there are a few exceptions, of which the most notable is Val Myer's 1932 design for Broadcasting House in London. The building was highly acclaimed and went on to become an icon of the then pioneering broadcasting age. Recognizing that part of that building's success could be attributed to its daring design at the time, the BBC wanted its new building to encapsulate a similar sense of adventure.

Naturally, acoustics were to play a key role, and, working with the masterplanners, the BBC commissioned Arup Acoustics in 2001 to develop the acoustic element of the brief. They collaborated with the BBC Symphony Orchestra and the BBC Singers to define what the performers themselves wanted from the building, and what the acoustic characteristics would be. It was particularly important to determine the core dimensions of the two spaces, one a rehearsal and performing area for the symphony orchestra, and the other a rehearsal room for the singers. As would be expected from FOA, even when constrained by complex requirements they have produced an exciting and refreshing design. The form resembles a vast aluminium extrusion with a glazed end that temptingly reveals some of the inner workings.

The BBC had the same facilities at Maida Vale but they were out of date and too

small, which restricted audience size. The requirements for recording and performing are complex and often at odds, the main difference being that recording requires very 'dry' or acoustically neutral conditions whereas a performing space needs to be more reverberant. The decision was made to design primarily for a performing space but to build in the versatility to permit certain types of recording. When a recording of an orchestra is made the engineers will place microphones close to the orchestra to capture the direct sound, but also others high up to catch the reverberant sound. The two sounds are then mixed to produce the required effect, but this is never an accurate recording of the actual acoustics in a building. The acoustic engineer has played a significant role in the design, to ensure that the building can be successfully used in both ways.

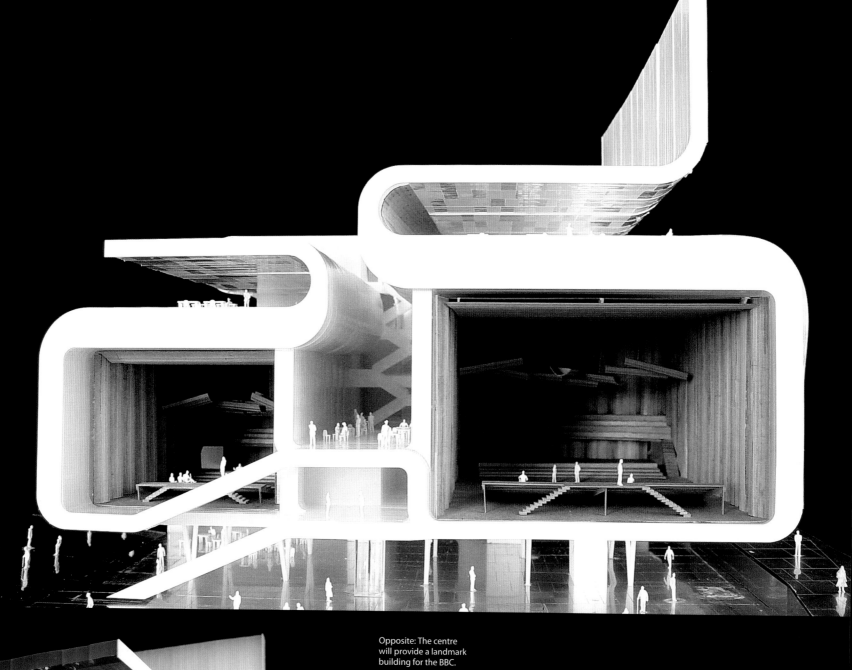

Opposite: The centre will provide a landmark building for the BBC.

Above: FOA's extruded form is a refreshing design. The outer layer wraps around and under the two auditoria, which are separated by circulation spaces, and emerges at the top of the building to frame terraces and bar areas.

Left: The building is supported by slim pillars and appears to hover a little way above the ground, creating a transparent ground floor.

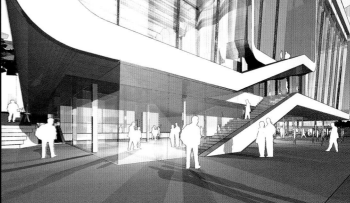

Left: The aluminium skin doubles as a projection wall, so that those outside can be included in the performances taking place inside.

Above, from top: The building is part of the planned new Media Village; carrying the weight of the upper storeys on a cantilever allows the foyer walls to be entirely of glass; the auditorium's clear end walls allow views out and in, another way of including those not present at a performance.

Client
British Broadcasting Corporation/Land Securities Trillium

Capacity
600

Area
6500 sq. m/70,000 sq. ft

Cost
£22m/$40.5m/€32m

233

FURTHER READING AND RESOURCES

Leo Beranek,
Concert Halls and Opera Houses:
Music, Acoustics and Architecture,
New York 2003

Deborah Borda and Frank Gehry,
Symphony: Frank Gehry's Walt Disney
Concert Hall, New York 2003

Philip Drew,
Sydney Opera House, London 2002

John McKean,
Royal Festival Hall, London 1993

World Architecture News
WorldArchitectureNews.com

Arup
www.arup.com/acoustics

Allies and Morrison
alliesandmorrison.co.uk

Paul Andreu
paul-andreu.com

Arte Jean-Marie Charpentier
arte-charpentier.com

Arts Team
artsteam.co.uk

Santiago Calatrava
calatrava.com

Christian de Portzamparc
chdeportzamparc.com

Dixon Jones
dixonjones.co.uk

Foreign Office Architects
f-o-a.net

Foster and Partners
fosterandpartners.com

Gregotti Associati International
gregottiassociati.it

Grimshaw
grimshaw-architects.com

Zaha Hadid
zaha-hadid.com

Haworth Tompkins
haworthtompkins.com

Henning Larsens Tegnestue
hlt.dk

Jakob + MacFarlane
jakobmacfarlane.com

Kohn Pederson Fox
kpf.com

KSS Design Group
kssgroup.com

Daniel Libeskind
daniel-libeskind.com

Moshe Safdie and Associates
msafdie.com

Richard Murphy Architects
richardmurphyarchitects.com

O'Donnell + Tuomey
odonnell-tuomey.ie

OMA
oma.nl

Dominique Perrault Architecte
perraultarchitecte.com

Renzo Piano Building Workshop
rpbw.com

Snøhetta
snoarc.no

Capita Percy Thomas
capitasymonds.co.uk/whatwedo/buildingdesign

Shin Takamatsu Architect & Associates
takamatsu.co.jp

UN Studio
unstudio.com

Rafael Viñoly Architects
rvapc.com

Von Gerkan, Marg & Partner
gmp-architekten.de

Michael Wilford & Partners
michaelwilford.com

Keith Williams Architects
keithwilliamsarchitects.com

6–7: Eujin Goh. 14–15: Brook Collins/ Chicago Park District. 22: Peter Guthrie. 28–29, 30t, 31: Didier Boy de la Tour. 32, 33, 34tl, 34tc, 34tr, 35 (all), 36–37: Richard Bryant. 61 (both), 62 (all), 63 (both): Martin Charles. 64–65, 66, 67 (both): Eujin Goh. 68–69: © Peter Aaron/ESTO, all rights reserved. 70tl, 70tr: © Peter Mauss/ESTO, all rights reserved. 71: © Peter Aaron/ESTO, all rights reserved. 72–73: © Alan Karchmer/ESTO, all rights reserved. 74, 75 (both): Michael Hammond. 77: © Alan Karchmer/ESTO, all rights reserved. 79, 80, 81: Nacása & Partners/Atsushi Nakamichi. 82b, 83tl: Hufton & Crow. 83tr: © Arts Team. 84bl: Derek Kendall. 84r (all), 85: Hufton & Crow. 86–87: Chris McGuire/City of Chicago. 88–89: Brook Collins/Chicago Park District. 96 (both): © Arup. 99, 100b, 101 (both): Peter Guthrie. 102, 103, 104–105, 106tl, 107: Nigel Young/Foster and Partners. 120, 121, 122 (both): Michael Hammond. 123: © Nick Guttridge/ESTO, all rights reserved. 124bl: Christian Richters, courtesy of Office for Metropolitan Architecture. 124–25: Charlie Koolhaas, courtesy of Office for Metropolitan Architecture. 124bl, 126tl, 126tr, 126cl: Christian Richters, courtesy of Office for Metropolitan Architecture. 127 (both): Charlie Koolhaas, courtesy of Office for Metropolitan Architecture. 128–29, 130–31 (both), 132 (all), 133: Wade Zimmerman. 134 (all), 135: © Douglas Friedman. 137, 138bl, 139tl, 139b: Philip Vile. 139tr: Will Mesher. 141: Hélène Binet. 142t: Hélène Binet. 144–45, 145 (both), 146tl, 146tr, 147 (all): Duccio Malagamba. 164, 165 (all), 166 (both), 168–69: © 2006 UN Studio. 170–71, 171t: Hayes Davidson. 171b: Charlotte Wood.

The publishers have made every effort to trace and contact copyright holders of the illustrations reproduced in this book; they will be happy to correct in subsequent editions any errors or omissions that are brought to their attention.